Stepping Up!

How Christ Turned My Pain & Suffering Into Hope & Joy

Caitie Crowley, MS IDS

En Route Books and Media, LLC
St. Louis, MO

Make the time

En Route Books and Media, LLC

5705 Rhodes Avenue

St. Louis, MO 63109

Cover credit: Caitie Crowley

ISBN-13: 978-1-952464-95-9

Library of Congress Control Number: 2021943976

Dedication

For my nana & Deacon Roger, who listened to the promptings of the Holy Spirit & encouraged me.

For my mom & dad who never left my side.

Acknowledgments

Thank you to everyone who played a role in my journey and thank you to Almighty God for the honor of writing about You.

May God bless you all!

Contents

Introduction

Healing and Strength

Two words I've asked God to give me every day— two words that seemed too far out of reach just one year ago:

Life and death.

Two words we all know well, yet they don't really sink into the everyday vocabulary. Death, especially. Nobody wants to think about it, and I can't blame them. It can be scary. Who wants to think about death until old age? Shouldn't you have many peaceful years of bliss? Or, if you are a good person, you try to be kind to people and go to Mass on Sundays. That's good, right? Or, if you're like me, you think you are taking your faith to the highest level by going to weekly Mass, adoration, and bible study. That's all you really need to live a good God-centered life. Right? Well, what happens when you become Simon of Cyrene and a cross is forced on you that you didn't sign up for? What if life and death are looking at you straight in the eye? What if all those years of Catholic faith are going to be tested in ways you couldn't ever imagine?

It is sobering to think about the fact that I could easily not be here right now — that my life could have been over in one moment or that I could have become vegetative. Both are downright terrifying. I know now I am a miracle, and I am grateful to Almighty God for it. It is amazing to think that nobody who randomly saw me on the street would ever know this about me.

As I am writing this, I can't believe it's been a year since my traumatic car accident. During these 12 plus agonizing months, I desperately wanted time to pass, but it never seemed to move fast at all. These pages will take you through my experience and my take-aways from it. Through Christ, I'm proof you can turn pain and suffering into hope and joy.

Part 1

The Initial Impact

On the morning of May 22, 2019, I was simply Caitie Crowley — a graduate student at Northwestern and a project manager at a marketing company where I managed clients such as Caterpillar and LG Seeds. I exercised usually six days a week doing either high-intensity cardio or weightlifting to stay in shape, which started when I competitively danced in high school. However, in the afternoon of May 22, 2019, I became a trauma patient: "Young adult female… difficulty breathing… coughing up blood… appearing to have multiple broken bones with complaints of severe pain in left arm and leg." Suddenly, I had lost my identity.

To back up a little bit, I was driving home early from work on May 22 around 2 p.m. It was a clear and sunny day. I was taking my normal route home from work like any other day. As I was driving on the interstate, one moment was ordinary and the next in a split second a car was coming right at me. I was so startled to see someone there as I was in the right-hand lane. I looked to the left and saw that no car was next to me, so I maneuvered to the left. That's when my car started tipping. Then it was as if someone took hold of my steering wheel and forcefully cranked it to the right. The car seemed to drive itself for a split second. During this point, which was a matter of seconds, I felt great anxiety at a level I hope to never know again. That's when my car started rolling. The level of pain I felt as my car was being smashed on its roll-overs was indescribable. I was alert this whole time. It was excruciating and terrifying. I thought for sure I was going to die.

As soon as my car started to roll, I said, "Jesus, I am so sorry. Jesus, I am so sorry for my sins." I repeated this again and again and again. I felt as though I was in slow motion. I couldn't remember the Act of Contrition, but I hoped that Jesus knew I tried so hard to live a life for Him. I thought about how much I would miss my family. I was saddened that I was never going to get married as I had so greatly longed for.

After the rolling stopped, I thought I was going to see Jesus, but instead my car landed facing the oncoming traffic. There was a strong smell of gasoline. I was sitting somewhat upright, but my left leg was dangling out of the left window, or where there used to be a glass window. The pain was burning all over my entire body; blood was everywhere, and my clothes were ripped. I looked to the left and noticed a woman and man next to my window.

The woman was near tears and cried, "I saw your left leg… your whole body was almost flying out the window."

The man cut her off and stated, "Can you tell me your name?"

I answered, "Caitie Crowley."

He asked, "What did you have for breakfast?"

I replied, "Mini Wheaties with a banana."

He asked me a few other questions, but the pain was so bad I was having more difficultly in answering. Plus, I kept coughing up a large amount of blood.

He prompted, "Caitie, keep talking to me. The ambulance is on its way."

The woman exclaimed, "We should try to move her."

He firmly answered, "No, nobody is touching her."

The woman asked me for my mom's phone number, and by some grace, I was able to recite it. She called my mom to tell her I was in an accident and to go the hospital. She held my hand and asked if she could pray for me. I said yes, and so she did.

The ambulance with first responders arrived. One of them immediately climbed on top of my car and said, "We are going to get you out of here. Hang tight."

I asked, "Should I try to move?" As I asked, I tried to sit up, but my body didn't move at all. It just laid there limp, which alarmed me.

He firmly stated, "No, don't move."

They used the jaws of life to cut down my door, get me out and on a stretcher with a neck brace, and then put me into the ambulance.

"Are you taking me to OSF?" I asked. I wanted to be certain I was going to my Catholic hospital that is a Level 1 Trauma Center.

"Yes," one of the responders answered. "Tell me what hurts?"

It was extremely difficult to speak as I felt like I couldn't breathe and was coughing up more and more blood. "My leg," I moaned.

"The left one?" they inquired.

"Yes," I confirmed.

"What else?" they asked.

"My left arm." I sighed.

"What else?" they asked again.

"It hurts to breathe," I choked.

They immediately put a suction tube in my mouth. I could feel the ambulance speed picking up. It felt like we were rocking and shaking—not a real smooth ride.

Then the main first responder, a heavy-set man, was crouched over me and yelled, "God d***!" "What?" another one spoke up.

"I keep blowing her veins, God d***," the same responder angrily said.

"Did you try here?" the other one asked pointing at a spot on my arm.

"Jesus, yes I did, dammit," he responded.

It was really upsetting me to hear this. Am I dying? It sure felt like it. Between the shaking of the ambulance vehicle and the fact that my entire body felt like it was on fire, I thought I was going to pass out. I think the kind responder noticed and said, "Here, I've got it," as he inserted my IV stick. "Hang in there," he continued, "We are almost there."

After what seemed like forever, although it was probably only 10 minutes, I was rushed into OSF Saint Francis' Emergency Department and more specifically the trauma bay. I was immediately assessed, put into a hospital gown, and rushed to get an MRI to fully identify my injuries. I glanced over at the team of nurses and doctors working on me, and I recognized one doctor even amidst my excruciating pain.

"Omg," I thought to myself, "This is freaking awkward. I matched with that guy on Catholic Match! Something awkward *would* happen to me. I hope he doesn't recognize me. This is so weird." Luckily, he was too busy to notice.

I was taken back to the trauma bay, put on oxygen, and started on pain meds. The meds didn't help at all. I still wasn't yet told what my injuries were when one of the medical staff asked, "Would you like to see someone in pastoral services? We have Pastor so and so here."

I still thought I had the potential of dying since I couldn't breathe easily and was still coughing blood, so I exclaimed, "I need a priest! I want Last Rites."

"Okay, sure thing," she nodded.

She sent the priest in, and he commented, "So what you do need? You asked to see a priest?"

Here I was completely black and blue with blood everywhere, laying limp with burning pain all over my body. Yes, excuse me for wanting a priest in case I die!

"I want Last Rites," I stated.

"Well, my shift is technically over, but since I'm here, I'll do it." So, he begrudgingly gave me last rites and left. I didn't feel consoled at all, but I hoped that he did the rite correctly and that it had given me some graces.

Soon after, my parents came rushing into my room. "Honey, we're here," my mom said, immediately grabbing my hand.

The attending doctor came over and said to us, "Caitie, you are going to be fine, but you have a long, tough road ahead of you. No brain damage or spinal cord damage whatsoever. However, you have contused lungs, a broken left collarbone, broken left elbow, multiple knee injuries, including ACL, PCL, meniscus, tibial plateau, plus left ankle on both sides, one left toe, and one right finger. We need to operate on the knee and ankle and possibly the elbow. I am going to reduce your leg in the interim until we can get surgery scheduled. Did you play sports at all?"

My mom answered, "No, but she was a dancer."

"Ooh," he sighed shaking his head, "This is going to take a lot of grit to get through all this."

He gave me more pain meds, and then straightened and aligned my leg. The pain was absolutely horrible. I prayed to God and offered up my suffering but begged him to take my pain away. I had no idea that this pain was just the beginning.

Impact Reflections: One year later

Trust in the Lord with all your heart... It will be a healing for your flesh and a refreshment for your body.

~Proverbs 3:5,8

Looking back, I never in a million years thought something like this would ever happen to me. I never thought that I would get into a car accident as I am a responsible driver; however, I didn't anticipate that someone else's bad decision could be the start of it. Never in another million years did I think I would not have great physical health. That my body wouldn't do what I wanted it to do. That I would have to become dependent on others. I thought that was only supposed to happen in late old age, not to a 24-year-old. My life was just beginning.

I would have never anticipated my life changing early on that day, May 22, 2019. I had fresh hair highlights and freshly painted toes. It was a warm, sunny, spring day. I had on a cute new outfit that went perfectly with my sterling silver cross necklace. I was on top of all my projects at work. I was caught up on my Northwestern graduate coursework. I was going to take a long weekend. It was also my Aunt Kate's birthday, and my family and I were supposed to meet her and her family for dinner to celebrate. Unfortunately, nobody made it to dinner that night. My mom was in the middle of baking cupcakes when she saw that she had 10 missed calls and two voicemails in the matter of a few minutes. My dad was working when he saw that he had several missed calls and voicemails. My parents were able to call my nana, my brother, and our extended family to let them know that I was in the Emergency Room.

Looking back at the impact itself, in the few minutes before it happened, I saw it as just an ordinary day. There is no way to anticipate someone else's not using the roadways the way they are intended and the way we were taught in driver's ed. While it was happening, I truly thought it was the end for me. However, I am so grateful that my first thought was to pray to Jesus. I believe the Holy Spirit prompted me to do so. I also think my guardian angel helped to protect me as well.

I later learned that my air bags did not actually deploy in my vehicle; there isn't any explanation as to why I didn't have any brain or head injuries. The design experts who evaluated my car and the rollover are perplexed as to how I survived—perhaps Carrie Underwood's song, *"Jesus, Take the Wheel,"* may help you understand. I also had a blessed medal from my grandpa in my car that unfortunately was lost during my accident. However, I was so grateful that it was with me during my time in need. I have since bought and had a priest bless another one for when I get another car.

Several months after my accident, I was able to meet the man, Randy, who came to my rescue. He saw the whole accident unfold as he too was leaving work early that day. He was in the car on the exit behind the man who started my accident. He saw the other driver take the wrong exit, turn around on the ramp, go offroad, and come directly at my car. He immediately pulled over on the shoulder of the road and ran toward me. He said that he didn't know what he would find when he got to my car and that he will never forget that day as long as he lives.

Two other witnesses corroborated his story to the police officer. He told me that several good Samaritans stopped and ran out into the intersection to gather my things like my backpack, sunglasses, etc. He asked me if I had a concussion, and I told him no. He said he wasn't surprised. He is an engineer and also a trained first responder. Based on his preliminary assessment, he thought I would be okay. After talking to him, I felt such great peace. At the time of the accident, I felt alone and abandoned by God. Where were you? I had asked Him several times in prayer. He had sent this man, a first responder, to follow behind me and to be there with me. I felt God's love in that moment.

A few months later, I was able also to meet the woman who had been standing next to Randy at the scene. Sadly, she changed from being concerned about me at the accident to defending the man who had caused it. She's the mother of his girlfriend. I am not going into any more details regarding this except to say that I identified with Jesus as he was betrayed by Judas. It is very sad, but everyone has free will, and all we can do is pray for them.

As for the Catholic Match doctor, he did eventually recognize me and had to meet my parents since he was helping to take care of me. I felt awkward at first, but now it is funny to think and laugh about. He is a great doctor and a good man. I am very grateful to him and all my doctors; I really felt like the Lord blessed me with the best of the best.

The feeling that most stands out from this initial impact was the extreme pain and fear. I also had no idea that those would linger quite a while before they would fade. I had to put my faith in God and trust that He would bring goodness out of this situation even though I couldn't see it in the moment. I only could start to see it as time passed. I remember watching an episode of Mother Angelica, foundress of EWTN, where she was talking about putting trust in God. She said, "God never said, 'Blessed are those who understand.'" I laughed because I always want to have a plan and know what I am doing and what is ahead. Yet, in this situation, I didn't understand any of it. God was just simply asking me to trust.

Now back to the hospital...

Part 2

Pain, Prayers, and Perseverance

I spent a few days in the Surgical ICU before moving to the Ortho floor. During this time, I had frequent breathing treatments and was on oxygen. The breathing treatment solution, which had a disgusting taste, sometimes leaked into my mouth.

I had daily labs in the middle of every night, which meant a new needle stick every night even though the ambulance tech blew all my good veins. On several occasions they had to re-stick blown veins, which really hurt. Many of them couldn't get me on the first try because my veins are hard to see. There is nothing quite like multiple, painful needle sticks at 3 a.m. I also had stomach shots twice a day to prevent blood clots.

My hair had matted into one rat's nest after it got caught in the neck brace from the scene of the accident. I couldn't be touched until I was more stable, so it stayed like that for a few days. It took my mom almost two hours to untangle my hair with a whole bottle of detangler, and she still had to cut out a few pieces. I would have had a panic attack if all my hair had to be cut off. Thank God that didn't happen.

I had to be on a bedpan for the first time in my life. That was humbling. I am normally a side sleeper but had to sleep on my back because I couldn't turn my leg. I had to sleep with my leg elevated with several ice packs to dull the pain. I had to sleep this way for a couple months and didn't sleep solidly through the night for about four months.

Amidst all this pain, fear, and uncertainty, I received so many flowers that we literally ran out of room. I also received tons of cards, texts, and family and friend visits. One of my parents was always by my side both day and night. One of the staff members said, "There is a lot of love in this room." That was certainly true. I also met a new friend, Jamie. She had had a traumatic car accident a year and a half before I did. She came and visited with her parents. They brought me a gift basket and gave such encouragement. I remember thinking that she looked totally normal and that I'll never be like that again.

Most importantly, I had prayers pouring out for me from families, prayer groups, and several churches and people I didn't even know. Plus, several Masses were said, and numerous candles were lit. Both of my parish priests came to visit me in the hospital, which gave me great strength. I asked and was given the Anointing of the Sick since my previous blessing in the ER was less than stellar. One of my priests, Father O'Brien, said, "Looks like God has a job for you." I also was able to receive the Eucharist every single day, which gave me great comfort.

My surgery was coming up, and my mom asked if the repairs could all be done under one anesthesia to lessen pain and risk. Four specialists were needed, and one of them was very rude and said he and the other surgeons were all busy with no way to coordinate their schedules. "She will have at least two anesthesias, maybe more," he said. Then my mom asked another of my surgeons, and he said, "Yes, absolutely, I will make it happen." He coordinated with all the surgeons, and they scheduled me for 6 p.m., which is after normal hours so that all of them were free.

I was very nervous waiting for surgery all day. I was still in extreme pain even with all the rest and pain meds, but I didn't think the pain could be worse because it was already bad. Well, I was wrong. When I was in recovery and waking back up, I had a severe PTSD attack from the drastic increase in pain. The details of this specific attack are fuzzy to me, but the nurse told my mom that I was crying and wanted someone to hold my left leg. The nurse was very kind and empathetic and held my leg for me until the episode passed. However, that was just the start of it. I went back to my room and spent nearly 10 hours with no increase in pain meds. So, I was on the same amount as before the surgery, and it wasn't even coming close to touching the pain. The trauma doctors were my attending physicians, and they did not have an order in for increased pain meds because they didn't communicate with the Ortho floor. It wasn't until I had a better morning nurse, Chris, that the pain would be properly managed. She contacted the trauma doctors to get the order. I also remember blacking out during these 10 hours because the pain was so unbearable.

The good news was the doctors told my parents that surgery went better than expected. Instead of multiple knee surgeries, they got all the injuries fixed in one. My ankle surgery went great. Only the medial side needed surgical repair. My elbow ended up not needing to be surgically repaired. The rest of the fractures were left to heal on their own. My parents also received the news that I wouldn't be able to weight-bear on my left leg for a minimum of 3 ½ months and that it could be longer depending on how it healed.

After my pain level became somewhat tolerable, physical therapy came to visit. This was the start of my unpleasant physical therapy experiences. One of them exclaimed, "Time to move!" as the other two just stared at me laying in my hospital bed.

I explained, "It's not that I don't want to move, but I don't think I am I able to. I can't hold myself up."

She shamed me and sneered, "You don't want to be on a bedpan for the rest of your life, do you?"

Another one jumped in and said, "Yeah, looks like you are going to always be stuck with a bed pan. How pathetic. Maybe you should be more motivated."

The other two cackled.

Immediately, my Aunt Kate and my mom said, "We need to talk to you in the hallway." They proceeded to tell the therapists that they aren't to talk to me like that ever again. The therapists left. One of them along with new one returned the next day.

"Okay, let's just try sitting on the side of the bed," she said. I was lying down with my head slightly elevated.

"I'll try," I replied.

Using my right arm, I tried to push myself up. I

was close to sitting upright when I started to fall back. Luckily. my mom was behind me, caught me, and helped support me back up.

"Great, now we want you to swing your legs to the side of the bed," one therapist said. I couldn't even hold myself up, but I guess they just ignored that.

"I can't lift my left leg at all; it is too heavy," I answered.

"I'll hold it," she replied.

I moved my right leg over. She started to move my left leg over and then suddenly dropped it. I felt a burning, stabbing pain pierce through the whole leg. She caught it right before it hit the ground. I started crying, the pain was so intense.

"What are you doing? She just had surgery," my mom exclaimed.

"I wanted to see if she could hold it up," the therapist answered.

Through my tears I cried, "I told you I couldn't hold it."

"Well, now we know for sure," she replied. Then she set my leg back on the bed and left.

I had to continue sitting on the side of the bed each day and eventually learn how to use a slide board to move onto a chair—and with extreme pain. Each time, my mom made sure that the therapist held onto my leg. My mom stayed right next to me every time in case she needed to help hold me up. I never knew how much of a blessing it is to have a mom who is a pediatric intensive care nurse until now.

Perseverance Reflections: One year later

Thus says the Lord...I have heard your prayer and seen your tears. I will heal you.

~Isaiah 38:5

The fact that I was being cared for was a small consolation. While I felt safe somewhat and that this care would help me get better, everything caused pain—both physical and mental. The health care workers who were empathic greatly stood out as did the ones who had no empathy whatsoever. During these difficult days, I kept trying to cling to God, but I could not see Him working at all. It was extremely difficult to pray. I thought I had a great relationship with God before my accident. But now my interior life seemed to have crumbled. I only could pray my Hail Mary's', Glory Be's, and Our Father's mixed with "God, please help me" and "Jesus, take this pain away from me." I would say these randomly throughout the day or at times when the pain spiked. I became disheartened because they didn't bring much relief.

I received a card from Jim, my Grandma Rosie's cousin who was like a brother to her. The front cover read, "Everything that happens in this life is a gift. Even as you struggle through this difficult time, you are gaining strength and wisdom that will help you further down the road." The card moved me. I asked God to give me strength, but at this point, I could not see this suffering as a gift. I can now say it was a gift. However, back then I wondered what was further down the road for me? I had no idea.

The shameful treatment by the therapists was horrible. I didn't include all the numerous insults I received from them, but they were uncalled for. It is easy for patients to lose their dignity if you have a caregiver who doesn't treat medicine as a vocation, that is, a calling from God. Without God, it is cold. I realize now that they wanted to take their own wounds and brokenness out on someone else, and I was just an easy target.

I want to point out the importance of having family support, especially for the vulnerable. I am blessed with an amazing, supportive, Catholic family.

I am blessed to have my immediate family; I am blessed I still have one grandparent living, my nana; I am blessed to have aunts, uncles, and cousins who have my back. I am shown love daily, and many of my family were there with me to be my advocates. It makes me sick to think about all those who are in hospitals and nursing homes alone. They have no one to check on them and make sure they are being treated with respect and dignity. Please pray for those with no family or where their family has abandoned them. I urge you that if you have someone in your family that you haven't talked to in a while, especially the young and the old, check on them, see if they need anything, and let them know that you love them.

I am also very grateful that Jamie came to visit me in the hospital that day. Her journey of suffering gave me much solace throughout my journey. It was re-assuring to know someone else my age had gone through a similar experience, and it helped me to not feel so alone. If she could get through it, I thought perhaps I could, too. Throughout my healing journey, she was awesome about answering all my questions and letting me know how she got through certain situations. I'm sure that when her accident happened, she had no idea that her suffering would be a source of strength for someone she hadn't even met yet. Suffering bears much fruit, so please remember that the next time you experience suffering.

My Aunt Kate, my Godmother and the one whose birthday I missed, also had a traumatic experience in Chicago when an apartment deck she and friends were standing on collapsed. Like me, she was in her 20s and was unable to walk for nine months. Her story and her suffering also gave me great support during my time of need. Who would have thought that her suffering would still be bearing fruit so many years later? So, do not be disheartened; remember God will turn your suffering into grace you can use later. For that, I am confident.

PTSD. It's something I never thought I would have to experience. I very much empathize with our military and others who suffer with it. I'm not sure if it ever completely goes away, but if you can identify what your triggers are and know how to mitigate them when they start to come, you can greatly reduce their effects. While I still am suffering from PTSD, the symptoms are much better now than they were back then because of time and God's grace.

At first, I didn't want to share the fact that I was experiencing PTSD with anyone except my mom because I thought it made me look weak. But when I started to open up to a few people I know, I actually found out that they also suffer with PTSD from different causes. A willingness to be open and honest with others allows you to truly share and then discover that you aren't alone. I want others to know that they are not alone in their suffering and that their suffering isn't their fault. Traumatic events happen, and they are scary and unfortunately leave marks on you. However, by God's healing grace, you can get through absolutely anything, "for nothing will be impossible for God" (Luke 1:37).

Now back to the hospital, back home, and into the unknown...

Part 3

Living in the Unknown

I spent 11 days in the hospital, and it was finally time to get discharged. I had very poor discharge instructions and was not really told what was ahead of me. I had no idea what my life would look like. I was not told a timeline, expectations, etc. I didn't know when I could return to work or school, let alone work out. One of my good friends, Rachael, was getting married in November, and I had hoped to be able to walk in hands free to her wedding. I had also wanted to attend her weekend getaway bachelorette party. That unfortunately did not happen. The only specific instruction I was told was that I wouldn't be able to weight-bear on my left leg for at least 3 ½ months. Since my left arm was broken along with my left leg, I was not able to do crutches immediately. Instead, I had to be in a wheelchair, which lasted for about 10 weeks. My dad and extended family made sure that my room was ready for me when I returned home. That included moving my furniture down to the main

floor bedroom and setting up a wheelchair ramp outside.

The drive home from the hospital was anxiety-
producing yet joyful. I had to sit across the back seat
with multiple pillows to elevate my arm and leg and
had to ride that way in the car for quite a while. I had
to sleep in a small single bed from my college days
because my actual bed was too big and too difficult for
me to get into. It took both of my parents and a gait
belt to do transfers from my bed to my chair because
I was a high fall risk.

On the third day of being home, I ran out of my
pain medicine. They didn't tell me that I was only
getting three days' worth of supply. I ran out and was
in excruciating pain from both the sharp drop off and
from my injuries and surgery. We called the on-call
doctor, but he wouldn't write a script for Norco, the
next level down of pain prescriptions, because all nar-
cotic pain med scripts must be handwritten, and he
didn't want to drive down to the hospital. My dad was
willing to drive down to get it, but the doctor refused.
He said to wait until my doctor's appointment the
next day. So, I went 12 hours with no pain medicine.
I asked for the Norco script like the on-call doctor had
said, and my doctor was super rude about it. He said
he would only write one script, one time, and that I

should be content with Advil or Tylenol even though I was only one-week post-surgery. "Other countries only give you three days of pain meds," he said.

Thank God I don't live in another country, and his PA was more empathetic to controlling pain. From the moment the accident happened, I had constant, excruciating pain for three months straight — that's a very long *2,160* plus hours of pain.

At that same appointment and every Ortho visit thereafter, I had to get x-rays to see how my injuries were healing. That meant each time I went they had to take off my splint, ace wraps, and brace to get down to my bare leg. Each time it was very painful. My elbow/collarbone sleeve was easily removable, which luckily wasn't as big of a deal. The first time getting x-rays was traumatic as the tech didn't know how to remove my leg splint and started yanking my ankle.

I cried out, "That hurts, that hurts, please stop."

The tech sternly answered, "This has to come off. Maybe I'll try to cut it." She clearly had no idea what she was doing, which made me more frightened. "Get the doctor. I want to talk to him," I stated.

"We don't need to bother him," she answered.

"Get the doctor. This hurts! Please get him," I insisted.

She begrudgingly left and brought him in.

"What's going on?" he asked.

"She keeps yanking on my ankle; it really hurts," I whimpered as I had tears in my eyes. "Here," he said calmly as he gently lifted it out.

"Thank you," I responded with gratitude.

"No problem," he replied as he walked out.

A couple of weeks later, I started to experience new pain in my leg. My doctor was worried that it could be a blood clot and ordered a Doppler study to be done that day. There was a severe thunderstorm going on, and the office that was going to perform this study didn't have a covered drop-off spot. Plus, the parking lot was not close to the door. My dad parked as close as he could and put an umbrella above me as my mom helped scoot me out of the car into the wheelchair. They put a garbage sack around my leg because I could not get it wet. Then I held the umbrella as my dad and mom pushed me through the pouring rain uphill to the door, getting completely drenched in the process. This totally symbolized my struggle up to this point. I felt the other people in the office staring at me. I think they felt bad for me like "Look at this poor girl in a wheelchair in the pouring rain." Or at least I'd like to think so.

When I finally got back to get the study done, the woman started to pull on my splint. Talk about a flashback to my previous Ortho appointment. I asked, "What are you doing?" She stated, "This has to come off for the study."

I asked, "How are you planning on getting it back on?" Splints are this fabric, bandage-like material that's dipped into water to make it more like a cast. If you rip it off, it isn't going to be formed to your leg or hold anything in place.

"Well, you could go back to your doctor," she answered.

"But then I'd have a 20-minute bumpy car ride, and I don't have an appointment," I responded. "Well, we can't do the study with it on," she replied.

"So how do you do this study?" I asked.

"I have to press along the back of your leg and knee with this device," she described. "This ain't my first rodeo."

"You can't touch my knee," I said. "That would hurt too bad."

"Then we won't be able to tell anything," she answered.

I was super nervous at this point but tried my hardest to use my logic. "I don't think this is a good idea. I'm going to skip it."

Mom asked her to take images she could get without removing the bandage, and she did begrudgingly.

When done she said we could use the back door where there was a drive-through area with a roof to protect from the elements.

My dad spoke up and exclaimed, "That would have been nice to know before we got here."

Basically, this appointment was a lot of anxiety for no reason, and the images the tech took showed I didn't have a blood clot after all.

For months, I had constant medical appointments. It started off with home health nursing coming to our house. After they realized my mom was a nurse, they signed off. My mom monitored my medicine schedule as I was on several different pain and blood clot prevention meds for quite some time. She also cleaned my knee wound and incision lines as they made me queasy to look at, especially with all the staples. My mom also helped assist me with all my physical cares. Not being able to physically care for myself and get ready by myself brought me great sorrow. However, I was grateful that my mom could do it instead of a stranger.

Home health physical therapy came, but it was limited what they could do because of my doctor's orders. I had burning back and hip pain from sitting so much, so I tried numerous icy hot packets that always seemed to fall off after an hour. I had a couple primary care appointments as well to make sure that my labs had stabilized, which they did. They also gave suggestions for my knee wound as it was deep with a high possibility for infection.

My family and friends' love and support continued during these first few rough months at home. Several meals, flowers, cards, visits, and prayers kept pouring out. Deacon Roger and his wife, Linda, visited me each Sunday to do a "mini mass" with that week's readings and brought me Jesus in the Eucharist. They also happened to be my 8th grade CCD Confirmation teachers, and that made their ministering to me extra special. The Holy Spirit was with them. I also received monthly First Friday visits from my two parish priests. They, too, brought the Eucharist and gave me consolation during a time of spiritual desolation.

The Unknown Reflections: One year later

So do not fear, for I am with you; do not be dismayed,
for I am your God. I will strengthen you and help you;
I will uphold you with my righteous right hand.
                                        ~Isaiah 41:10

I remember being so excited to come home because I thought that once I could get home in my own bed my pain would go away. While the constant lab sticks, bed pan, and stomach shots went away, the physical pain stayed ferocious for a long time. And that's even when I wasn't doing anything. Every appointment brought even more physical pain—from the pulling on my leg for examinations and x-rays to getting my staples out. Any movement of any kind brought pain; lying completely still brought pain. I couldn't escape it. I don't think I will ever forget that feeling.

With this burning pain, I could not stand to wear fitted clothing because I didn't want anything clinging to my skin, arm, or leg. I started off wearing some of my dad's button-down shirts, but after about a couple weeks of that, I couldn't stand to wear those anymore. So, I switched to wearing my mom's workout clothes. That worked out a lot better (pun intended). Her clothes were looser on me yet a bit more normal for me. I didn't start to wear my own clothes again for about three months; once I did, I only had a few pants that would fit over my leg brace. Adjustments in clothes do not seem like a big deal, and comparatively speaking they aren't. It was just another part of my life that had to be adjusted for a while.

Being in a wheelchair, however, definitely left a

lasting impression on me. Even now, I still get a deep, sorrowful sinking-in-my-stomach kind of feeling when thinking about my time in the wheelchair. It was only 10 weeks, but it truly felt like 10 *years*. And even beyond the 10 weeks, I still had to use the wheelchair to get out of my house for several more weeks because I couldn't do stairs with my crutches. It was a difficult pill to swallow. When you see someone in a wheelchair, help that person if he or she needs it; also say a quick prayer for him or her. These individuals are warriors, but they need prayers to strengthen them as there are very tough days.

Being in a wheelchair was one of the most eye-opening experiences of my life. I always felt bad for people in them. I always thought it was sad. But now my heart breaks for those individuals who don't have legs that can support them. I also realized how much we cannot take our health or our legs for granted. At any moment we too can become disabled. It is not just for the poor souls who are born that way. Being in a wheelchair taught me humility. Each time you go out in public, people stare. In those moments, I felt like I would never escape the wheelchair. Beyond the staring, being in a wheelchair produces a lack of freedom. You can't go anywhere by yourself, or at least not easily. Just to leave my house took so much effort. I had to transfer to the chair, have a parent push me down the ramp (only had one functional arm), wheel me to the car, and transfer me to the car. Then, a parent would have to load the wheelchair into the trunk, which always took about five attempts before it would fit and close, at least for my dad. Then we'd drive to wherever and hope our destination would be wheelchair accessible. Being sedentary also causes a lot of pain. The body was meant to move; when it can't, pain and atrophy set in very quickly.

When I heard the news that I couldn't weight-bear for at least 3 1/2 months, that seemed like three years. A lot of fear emerged: How can I *not* do anything for that long? How can I *not* exercise for that long? What if I get fat? What if I go stir crazy? I was used to a minimum of five solid workouts a week; I didn't even count my Sunday walks with my family and dog as a workout; I just counted that as a few extra steps and nice to be outside type of a thing. What if I can't ever do a workout class again? That was my stress management. Now in the most stressful time of my life I can't rely on exercise to help me. The last time I went a week without working out was when I was too young to remember. I started dancing as a little girl and replaced dancing after college with classes like Zumba, circuit training, step, and weightlifting. And yet I had to accept it. Even though I knew my body could not do it, I still really missed it.

Kay, one of my YMCA instructors who taught RIPPED, which includes a variety of circuit training, sent me a card and gift card on a day that I was particularly discouraged about not being able to work out. The front of the card read, "Even small steps will get you where you are going." It really struck me. She had a very sweet note and ended it with Isaiah 41:10. She had also underlined the word strengthen. I had been praying to God for strength, and I felt the Holy Spirit working through Kay to remind me that He was with me and was strengthening me.

It was during these times that I really learned to take it one day at a time. That is all I could do. I really longed for the day I could start to learn to walk again, but that was in the unreachable distance. My days pretty much consisted of rest in between constant medical appointments. Those became not only physically draining but mentally draining as well. However, the one thing I really looked forward to each week was receiving the Eucharist. It always made me feel better. I remember one particular conversation I'd had with one of my parish priests, Father Henehan.

"Why did this happen to me?" I asked him when I was seeking spiritual direction.

This is a paraphrase, but he said, "I can't directly answer that question, but I know that God brings good out of every evil. He did not cause your accident, but He permitted it. Think of the image of a rock. There are two ways to mold it. The first is to slowly run water over it over time. This is like the wisdom you gain over a lifetime. The second is to forcefully hammer it. This way hurts, but you are given fast, immediate knowledge. You are experiencing the hammer. You've been given insight that others cannot see.

"Suffering teaches us many things. You understand what is really important, and we would become selfish if God gave us everything we want. The closer you are to Christ, the more you share in His cross. Who is the person Jesus is closest to? Mary. He shared the most suffering with her. Suffering can make people better or bitter; it is your choice. You can make this time about growing in holiness or in turning away from God."

I eagerly told him that I want to grow in holiness, and I honestly did my best attempt at it during this trial and the trials ahead. Father also recommended great spiritual books by Father Walter Ciszek and Father Jacques Philippe on suffering and the interior life, and they really helped me as well. He also told me to offer up my suffering each day for a particular person to give that day's suffering meaning, and so I did. That was my prayer life for several months. It wasn't until around month seven or so when the burdens started to lift that I was able to start having deep conversations with God again. The key here is persistence. Even if your entire being feels like you can't pray, pray anyway. In any form. In any way that you can muster. Please pray. Even for one minute. You don't have any idea how much grace is poured out in that moment.

In addition to the Eucharist, spiritual direction, and spiritual reading, I also invoked the help of many saints along my journey. I thought I needed a team of people to pray for me because I really needed a miracle. I started with St. Bernadette as she was my confirmation saint. My nana bought bottles of Lourdes water to give to me, and I religiously put the water all over my leg and arm for months. If you aren't familiar with her story, the Blessed Mother appeared to a poor French girl, and one time she asked her to dig into the ground and a spring of water appeared. Thousands of pilgrims travel to Lourdes, France, for this healing water, and many people have been cured of their illnesses. I also asked Mother Mary, St. Joseph, St. Jude, St. Rita, and soon to be St. Fulton J. Sheen to intercede for me. I call them the dream team: The mother of God, Jesus' foster father, St. Jude for impossible cases, St. Rita for physical healing, St. Bernadette for healing, and my hometown St. Fulton J. Sheen. Can't get much better than that! I highly encourage you in your time of need to call upon the saints. They are your friends, and they want to pray for you. I was also really struggling to pray for myself, so I knew that they could pray better than I could. That brought me comfort knowing I could trust in their prayers.

Now back to physical therapy and figuring out a new normal…

Part 4

Physical Therapy, More Physical Suffering

In July, I started physical therapy with my first physical therapist. I was in a wheelchair and non-weight-bearing; I was a complex patient no doubt. The physical therapist said it would take time, but he would get me back to walking. I was able to progress to crutches around 10 weeks later. I was very unstable with them, which meant I needed one of my parents with me when I tried to walk. Even though it was a great struggle, and I couldn't go far on them at all, crutches finally relieved my back and hip pain. The leg and arm pain still persisted. In total, I was non-weight bearing on my left leg for 13 ½ weeks (this was because the doctors were fearful that the platform they built up for my tibial plateau could re-shatter), and I was not 100% weight bearing until 4 ½ months.

Around August, I was able to make many basic milestones. I returned to my normal bed, started sleeping on my side, got off all medicine, got rid of the gait belt, got rid of the slide board, got rid of the wheelchair, lowered my left leg to the ground and tolerated it, regained full range of motion including hyperextension on my arm, sat normally in a car, got rid of the splint, and went into a knee and ankle brace but didn't have to wear them when sleeping.

While the physical therapist gave me a couple of exercises that helped, he never wanted to talk about PT. He was actually condescending and talked about retirement and the different women he "comforted" before his second marriage. Since I was vulnerable, I put up with these creepy stories in the hopes he'd get me walking again.

However, once I finally got weight-bearing privileges, he told me after one week of my using two crutches to use only one crutch. I said I felt unstable and off-balance, and he said do it anyways. He took one of my crutches and put it across the room and said, "Go fetch." I took a few steps with the one crutch slumped over, and then my knee gave out. Also, I found out later from my doctor I was in the wrong brace. Plus, I was given only range of motion exercises at this point, no strengthening exercises. I almost fell but managed to catch myself as he refused to use a gait belt on me or stand next to me.

Because of this awful experience, I asked to get a

referral to aqua therapy. There too I was shamed by a physical therapy assistant for not being able to walk in the shallow end. She told me that I must have a "mental block" and that I should be able to run by now.

After that "fun," I tried going to a different physical therapist at a different office. This was end of November into early December. Unlike the previous two therapists, this one was kind, but he tried to put me on a treadmill after only a couple sessions. I told him that would be too hard, and he told me to try. I only managed to be on it moving for about 60 seconds before about falling again.

So, now I had two physical therapists and one physical therapist assistant who had no grasp on the severity of my injuries. Instead of admitting that, they decided to shame me. Their comments were discouraging, but, more importantly, I could have been seriously hurt doing exercises that were too advanced for my injuries. God definitely must have been looking out for me.

As all these months were unfolding, my world was literally and figuratively turned upside down; it was difficult to grasp. Nothing looked the same anymore. Even when I was trying my absolute best, it didn't feel like it was getting any better. Those days felt like they would never end. One day was really no different from the next. I tried to create a routine even though there really wasn't a routine to be had. This helped me cope, especially during the days of no weight-bearing. Plus, I think it helped me even more with healing. It made me feel productive and in control of something.

So here are the practical tips that I implemented during this unpleasant time and continue to do to this day:

1. Start the day off in prayer. Each morning I thank God for another day, and I truly mean it.

No day is guaranteed at any age. In the early days, my prayer was "Lord help me. Amen." That's all I could muster at the time. It started to expand once I picked someone each day to offer my sufferings for. I eventually moved into more conversational prayer of thanking God for the things going well and praying about the things not going well, etc. Each day I also prayed for healing and strength—physically, mentally, emotionally, and spiritually—because this experience was a battle. I also try to pray sporadically throughout the day and thank Jesus throughout the day, too.

2. Move every single day. In the beginning, I had about four PT exercises that took less than 10 minutes

because that's all I was cleared to do. So, I would do those and then shower for the day. Sadly, that was enough to tire me out. Eventually, I moved to doing an hour or two of PT a day plus tried to move around after sitting for a while. Movement is good for the mind, body, and soul.

3. Get outside as much as weather allows. I have a beautiful backyard with a fountain. I would sit either on the back deck or the sunroom. In the beginning, my mom would wheel my wheelchair outside for me to get some fresh air, and it really helped renew my spirit. Now, I go for walks outside. I get my steps in and get a renewed perspective.

4. Do activities as tolerated. In the beginning, I didn't have energy to do anything. I didn't even have energy to talk. I felt bad because many people visited or wanted to talk on the phone, and I would simply wear out. That lasted for several months. I started off watching TV and movies around the clock. I eventually got sick of that and started reading. Once class started up again, that really helped structure my day. Pace yourself and learn to be gentle with yourself.

5. Go places when you feel like it. I am very much a homebody, but I eventually did get cabin fever. For several weeks, I didn't want to go anywhere because I

had constant appointments that tired me out. I simply didn't have energy for it. Eventually, my parents took me on car rides. I also met friends for coffee, lunch, etc. However, I was very much harped at by my first physical therapist to go out to dinner and be busier. But I think that as long as you get out sometimes, that is fine. Don't let others push you when something is too taxing.

6. Set small, realistic goals. I tried to set small goals and add to them over time so that I felt like I was making progress. When you can't hold yourself up in bed, your goal can't be to walk. That is too big of a jump. Breaking down long-term goals into short-term ones helps you to persevere and see it through to the end.

7. Document the process. It was my mom's idea, but I actually kept a journal of my milestones. At first, it seemed pointless, but over time it was amazing to go back and read how far I had come. Especially on the days I was more than usually discouraged about what I could not do, I had a physical reminder of what was once impossible and now was possible.

Suffering Reflections: One year later

Rejoice in hope, endure in affliction, persevere in prayer.

~Romans 12:12

During this time, I experienced great frustration, and I felt hopeless. I couldn't do much by myself. I desperately was wishing for my old life back. I had to learn how to do everything completely differently. Eating, showering, what to do with my day, how to use assistive devices. There were several long, dark days. I felt it wasn't fair that everyone else could move on with their lives, but I couldn't. I craved the ordinary, but it wasn't within reach. Recovery is an extremely slow process that I wasn't prepared for. Many people didn't understand why I wasn't back to my old self by now or why I couldn't do certain things simply because they were too difficult. I also never realized how many places are not set up for people who struggle with mobility.

It also is gut wrenching for me to think about how helpless and vulnerable I was during this time. I was so desperate to walk again that I kept trying different options, but none was working. I couldn't understand why God wasn't having it work out. In hindsight, I think the Lord was teaching me perseverance. The devil definitely tempted some of my health care workers to be mean spirited, but the Holy Spirit prompted several others to show me empathy and compassion. What gave me consolation is that He was with me, and he sent me some very special people to walk this journey with me.

In hindsight, one of the best things I did during this time was aqua therapy. I still don't think very highly of the physical therapy assistant, but the water helped me significantly. I was able to do many exercises in the water that I couldn't do on land. I couldn't even hold myself up the first time in the water; the water was up to my shoulders, and I needed a safety vest. The second time I was able to move by holding onto a floating device. The third time I could be in the water without anything. Over time, my posture and coordination came back, and I also think it gave me the strength to make it to one crutch in the months ahead. Because these weren't super big changes, I couldn't feel the immediate benefit, but it was forming. It took me four months until I could walk in the shallow end with the water below my waist. That was a thrilling day.

Another thing that really helped was my seven steps; they helped me organize my day and organize my thoughts. They provided structure to my unknown waters. When everything seems out of control and ever changing, it is important to remind yourself God is unchanging, and it is important to give yourself practical tools to help make sense out of the chaos.

It is a lot easier to focus on the cruelty in the world than to focus on the light. But discouragement is what the devil wants. So, remember to try to look past the negative and to look for the positive. This doesn't mean to not recognize the difficulty. Trust me. I did have plenty of doubt and many dark days. Remember He is there; you just might have to look a little bit closer to see.

One blessing that happened during this time was that I was able to return to Mass in October. That was such a huge blessing, and I felt so extremely grateful to be strong enough on the crutches and brace to go. During the entirety of my trial, the Eucharist was an anchor to me. While I endured much difficulty, He gave me strength. It was also so wonderful to be welcomed back to Mass by my parish family. Several people came up and hugged me and said welcome back. It was a beautiful Mass and a beautiful day.

I was also able to return to graduate school in the fall. As it's an online program, I could do it from home. This was a real God-sent gift as it gave me a sense of normal and gave me something else to think about. I was also very blessed that a classmate of mine, Fawzia, did my portion of our group project when my accident happened back in May. That way I was able to finish the class and not have to retake it. My professor was also very understanding. Luckily, the class was almost over except for the final project, so my professor gave me my grade based on how I did up to the accident, which was an A.

During this time, I was also offered my dream job. I didn't even apply for it but was offered a job at a Fortune 100 company in my favorite division in my dream role. However, I couldn't take it. There was no way I could work 40 hours a week in-person. It was pretty crushing. I was also offered a full-time role at Students for Life of America, which I also couldn't take. This was also a bummer as I was wanting to get more into the Pro-Life movement. During my recovery, I was in the running for two other full-time jobs that I also had to turn down. In December, I started working 10 hours a week for the marketing agency I worked at prior to my accident as that was all the time that I had to give with my therapy schedule. Before my accident, I had been so extremely focused on my career and job opportunities that this was an extra hard pill to swallow. To say "Lord, I trust You. I want and wish so badly that I could take these opportunities, but it is not Your will for me right now. Help me to trust that you will bring me another great opportunity once I'm well again."

Another positive aspect was that I was also able to make my friend Rachael's wedding in November. Not hands free like I wanted, but I was on crutches. That was an improvement from the wheelchair. Walking up to the entrance of the reception was slightly sloped, and it felt like I was climbing up Mount Everest, but I made it. I brought my mom as my "plus one," and it was fun to get dressed up and experience the joy of that day.

Now back to my medical care…

Part 5

Crossroads

As I described earlier, I wasn't getting anywhere with my physical therapists, and I wasn't getting clear answers from my doctor on why I wasn't walking yet or when I would be. I was still on two crutches with a knee brace; I could stand without my crutches but only for a few minutes. So, at the end of December my parents and I went up to see a well-known Chicago doctor for a second opinion. As soon as the doctor came in the room, he put his hand on my shoulder and said, "I am so sorry that you have had to go through this suffering, especially at such a young age." His empathy and compassion stood out. This was the first time in a long time that a medical professional had recognized my identity and my dignity. Not only did he reassure me that I was right on target with my progress, but he also told me that I wasn't behind. He gave me multiple, specific benchmarks: when I should be on a cane, when I should be hands free, when my circulation would fully improve, how to increase knee bend, how to work on strength, etc. Overall, due to the extent of my injuries, I was told that it would be at least a one-year long recovery with even more gains in the second year and up to five years total healing. He answered every single question I had in one appointment. He brought me hope.

At the same time, the doctor said one sentence that was particularly jarring, "Honey, I hate to tell you this, but you will never do competitive dance or run ever again."

As soon as he said those words, I had a flashback to all my dance accomplishments over the years. Starting in middle school, I was invited to join Junior Company, an exclusive studio dance group, and made middle school poms team in both 7th and 8th grade. I was the only freshman in my grade to make dance team at Dunlap High School, which included both performance and competition. My sophomore year I was awarded UDA All-American and qualified to perform in Rome. I did dance team all four years, and every year we qualified for IDTA/IHSA state.

After doing dance team all four years, I was also the lead dancer in the school musical, *All Shook Up*. I choreographed middle school poms try-out routines, choreographed another area high school's half-time routines along with choreographing Dunlap's half-time routines. I taught kids at dance camps, taught

Spanish classes how to salsa, and through the Freshman Advisory program taught freshman how to dance at homecoming. In undergrad, I was on the Orchesis Dance Company through Bradley University, and I was asked to be an assistant instructor at the most prestigious dance studio in the area, Peoria Ballet.

From the time I can remember, dance had always been a huge part of my life and what I was known for. Many people were shocked that I didn't go to a professional dance company or attend a college well-known for dance to major in it.

While I had taken a break from dance to pursue graduate school, I never thought I was going to be done with dance. I had planned to return to teaching, choreographing, or even to do local shows. However, within just one simple sentence, dance, the love of my life, was gone forever.

Since I was struggling to get to one crutch, my family and I were also trying to brainstorm what could help. I felt like I needed walking bars, but they are really expensive and take up a lot of room. A family member suggested that we put up railings. We have a long, narrow hallway in one area of the house that was the perfect spot for them. My Uncle Dan is an engineer and a carpenter, so he installed the railings for me. This was a huge blessing because I could practice walking with one crutch and holding onto the railing with my other hand. This gave me much more security. I also eventually practiced walking hands-free with the railings as well.

Shortly after that appointment and practicing with the railings, I was finally able to walk with one crutch around the house and be barefoot for the first time. I was able to completely care for myself physically. I was able to lower myself to the ground to sit on the floor. I was able to go upstairs for the first time to my old room. I was able to make and get my own food from the kitchen. I was able to get rid of my brace. I was able to wear jeans, leggings, and normal pants for the first time again. I was able to pick up items off the ground again.

I also was finally able to find a good physical therapist who was kind and had a better understanding of my injuries. With his guidance, I was able to build strength. At month nine, otherwise known as February 18, 2020, I took my first steps hands free… by accident. I was getting ready for the day in the bathroom, and I went to reach for something and realized I'd taken a couple steps. I tried doing it again and took a few more steps. I started sobbing and thanking the Lord. I said, "Thank you, Jesus!" Again and again and again. I also kept reciting the Glory Be. It was the best, most exhilarating experience ever.

By mid-March, I was able to walk hands-free, crutch-free, and brace-free consistently. The first public place I wanted to walk at was St. Jude Mass. I was able to walk up by myself for the first time to receive Communion that day; I almost cried. Previously, I had a Eucharistic minister bring me Communion at my seat. I realized in that moment what a privilege it is to be able to walk up to receive our Lord. How deeply personal that encounter is. He is offering Himself to me, Caitie Crowley, an ordinary girl from an ordinary place. In that moment, it is just Him and me. How sacred. This was also the last Mass that I was able to attend before the coronavirus canceled public mass for a while.

The timing of the coronavirus really sucked for me. I felt like I had already been in quarantine all year. Now granted, I was able to make a few events and visit with family and friends, but my life really had to be put on hold. I had waited to get my hair highlighted because I wanted to be able to walk into the salon hands free, and I did. I also got my nails done and joined a new Lenten Catholic bible study for young adults. However, I only attended twice because then everything was shut down for two and a half months.

I also want to note that I am not trying to be insensitive to those who suffered or lost someone to coronavirus; I am just expressing my frustration that after the year I had, this was just another disappointment.

A few weeks later, my contract was terminated at my marketing agency also due to coronavirus. Their workload had greatly dropped, and they couldn't afford extra staff, which was what I had become after my accident. I thought that I would be sad as I somewhat anticipated this happening, especially after having all those full-time job offers that I had to turn down previously. But surprisingly, I was honestly at peace with it. After being dumped by my serious boyfriend a month before my accident happened and all the pain and suffering of my accident, losing this job just wasn't important. There are plenty more opportunities to come; I am confident of that.

Crossroads Reflections: One year later

So I tell you, whatever you ask for in prayer, believe that you have received it, and it will be yours.
                                                    ~Mark 11:24

There truly is no feeling quite like that moment when you can fully see and fully know God's grace pouring on a situation. Just having a deep sense of peace, knowing it is fully in his hands and that He is taking care of you is a feeling of being "light on your feet" because the light is truly present. The fruits of suffering make the joy taste that much sweeter.

That is how I felt after my Chicago doctor appointment and finding the right physical therapist. I finally felt joy, and the height of it was when I was finally able to take my first steps. I had been longing every single day, in the worst way, to walk again, and I had to wait nine months for this moment. Talk about delayed gratification. I think many people take walking for granted; I know I did. If you have the ability to walk, the world is wide open for you. You can do the ordinary and the extraordinary! You can travel on vacation or travel to the grocery store. You can take different jobs or work the job you have. You can go anywhere or stay right where you are. The choice is up to you instead of chosen for you.

I never realized it, but many people are blind. Not literally, but they do not know how blessed they are; they feel bad about themselves if they can't go on vacation or get the latest iPhone. They do not see the gifts God has given them like health, the ability to work, the ability to come and go as they please, the ability to live their life. Most importantly, they don't see God right in front of them. How could they when they are so busy being so great?

Throughout this experience, I had to turn down jobs; I had to turn down dates; I had to turn down trips. While those were disappointing, I was most sad that I couldn't do simple things. I wanted to be able to make my own lunch. I wanted to be able to drive myself to Adoration. I wanted to walk my dog, Christmas. Most people my age would find those things boring. Yet that is what I longed for—the simple and the ordinary. I encourage you to try to find the joy in the simple things; a simple life is the best life. See the blessings surrounding you; they're there.

I also want to remind you that there is always somebody out there worse off than you are. During my journey, I didn't think that was the case. I certainly didn't feel that way. Then one day I was waiting in a PT office and saw a girl younger than I am, probably about 16 or 17 years old, and she too was on crutches. However, when I looked closer, I noticed one leg, below the knee, was amputated. My heart sank for this girl. She was so young to be going through this, and she had lived way less life than I had at 24. She seemed extremely nervous but was doing her best to be up-beat. Now, I'm not saying that this girl can't live a full, happy life because I believe that she most definitely will. But I am saying that she will face challenges her entire life—challenges that I won't. My cross is temporary, but she will always have a physical reminder of hers. It is all about perspective.

A major blessing throughout the entirety of this journey was that I was able to reconnect with many people I hadn't seen or talked to in a long time as well as get to spend quality time in person with so many family members and friends. Life moves at such a busy pace these days that it usually only slows down on holidays, if then. I am not going to name every single person because I think I could write an entire book on how much they all mean to me and how much it meant to connect with each and every one of them. They all brought the joy of Jesus to me when I certainly needed it. They brought me smiles and laughter, and I can't even begin to describe how much it helped me to endure my cross.

I also want to point out here the importance of kindness. Sadly, in our society, kindness is viewed as weakness, but that is how our Lord wants us to treat others. The kindness that I was shown in the latter half of my medical recovery, I believe, was the foundation for my ability to heal internally and to be able to forgive those who insulted me earlier. Kindness and forgiveness go hand and hand.

I especially want to emphasize here the importance of forgiveness. I was mistreated by many medical professionals, especially the physical therapists, a
handful of others, and of course by the man who
started all of this to transpire from his bad decision.
Forgiveness is a tough thing. I had to learn that forgiveness does not mean whitewashing. It does not
mean acting like it didn't happen or that what they did
was fine. Forgiveness means letting go of the anger
and sadness and the wishing that bad things happen
to them. Forgiveness means that you hope that they
can find the Lord and that they change their ways
before it is too late. It is trusting that the Lord will take
care of them and that they will be held accountable on
judgment day, but I need to leave that to God. I need
to will their good and pray they turn to God. So, to all
those that hurt me, by God's grace, I forgive you.

Now back to my rehabilitation and recovery...

Part 6

Staying the Course

Once I was walking hands free, I was released from my doctor. He said once physical therapy discharged me, then I was free to live my normal life. At this point, the only pain I had was in my knee. It was around a 2-3 pain level, but it was very tolerable. The next week I went to physical therapy like normal and was told to try to skip/jump, and that led to burning, slicing knee pain for a solid two months. The pain level consistently stayed at an 8-9. I tried Advil, icing, and compression sleeves, but none of it worked. I consulted with my doctor, and he advised to lessen up on the exercise and see if it would go away on its own. I waited two months, and it didn't go away. So, in May, I went back in to see my doctor and was finally able to get a cortisol shot. Unfortunately, it didn't really help. The funny thing was that I was kind of nervous about getting the shot, but it didn't hurt at all! I didn't even flinch a bit. My doctor even asked, "Do you feel it?" The shot was five slow seconds into me and five slow seconds out of me, but it didn't bother me at all. So, I realized that I have a much higher pain tolerance now, and that's a plus.

During that appointment, I was also instructed that I should only ever do low-impact exercises such as walking, biking, and swimming and to never do any jumps, running, hiking, intense lunges, or aerobic classes. I also needed to really limit stair usage. If I stayed away from these types of exercises, I would avoid pain and having to get a knee replacement. At that appointment, my doctor also recommended that I have a consultation with the primary trauma surgeon after he saw something on my x-rays. I was hoping that it wasn't anything serious, and I was hoping that if I needed surgery that it could be pushed off for a while.

In May 2020, my physical therapist said that my left quad and both hips were still weak but would improve with time. Since my walking gait was still off, I was compensating by twisting my back, which started to cause bad back pain. I had to keep working on correcting it. My knee bend measured at 125 degrees, which was the most it had been up to this point. Typical knees bend to 135 degrees. The doctor and physical therapist thought I would gain some more degrees but probably not much more. They said it shouldn't limit me, but it was annoying because it made it more difficult getting down to the ground or reaching for something in a low drawer.

I continued to do my exercises at home every single day to increase my strength. I also had been wanting to go to the pool, but they have all been shut down due to coronavirus. Since it was finally starting to get hot outside, though, my next door neighbor offered me to use their pool. It was so kind of them as I don't really know them very well. So, I was finally able to do my pool exercises for the first time in over two months. The downside was that I had to walk down several stone steps to get to the pool and another four steps to get into the pool. All these steps caused my knee pain to flair back up, so I wasn't able to use their pool too much.

Another goal I was working on was getting used to different types of floors and uneven ground. I never realized it, but very little is completely flat. Most surfaces have bumps and unevenness, which more easily throws off my gait. For example, I walked through grass for the first time when I went over to my neighbor's pool, and the thickness made it more challenging. I also took walks around my neighbor-hood to get used to uneven concrete. I also am continuing to increase my walking distance. St. Jude

Church set up outdoor Stations of the Cross during Lent, and when they were first set up, my parents and I drove by them because I didn't have good stamina or stability. However, after about a month, I was able to walk them. God's grace is amazing!

I also started doing counseling at a Christian organization, and I really love it. I am still suffering with PTSD and was hesitant to drive again. My counselor was very kind and insightful, and he helped me break down the fear of driving into small manageable goals. He has given me tools and techniques to combat the fear, and by the grace of God, I planned to drive again soon.

From a professional standpoint, my studies at Northwestern graduate school continue to go extremely well. Only one course and a capstone are left until I graduate. I really am proud of myself to keep going with my program despite all that's happening. I'm especially proud of getting A's in two tough IT courses that I was super nervous about taking even before my accident. It will be such an exciting day when I can walk across that graduation stage.

My younger brother graduated from Bradley University. Because of coronavirus, his ceremony was cancelled. So, instead a bunch of my family organized a car honking parade with balloons, music, and fun. I was able to stand and walk around my driveway holding my dog, and I don't think I have ever smiled so widely. I was thrilled for my brother, but I was also so elated that I could participate freely and be so carefree.

Staying the Course: Reflections

I continue my pursuit toward the goal, the prize of
God's upward calling, in Christ Jesus.
~Philippians 3:14

I'm not going to lie; I was discouraged by my knee setback. Who wouldn't be? I thought I was signed off on doctors and appointments. I wanted to be healed so I could move on. I had come such a long way, but it was frustrating. Why did my physical therapist push me so hard? Why didn't my doctor tell me my limitations up front? I understand that they probably didn't want to scare me or have me be too fearful to try, but it brings back negative feelings of being in the dark. Do I want to have knee limitations? No, I don't. But I would rather know what they are and learn what is good for it so that I can gain confidence in what I can do instead of lose confidence because of what I can't.

This whole year was all about getting back to basic

functionality, which is amazing. I can do so much, but it's nowhere near close to perfect. The important thing for me (and for you should you ever be going through a similar situation) is to remind myself to focus on progress not perfection. Some days this is easier than others. I want perfect. I want my body to do whatever I want it to. If I want to walk fast, I want to be able to. If I want to balance on one leg without pain, I want to be able to. My knee isn't what it was before, and I have to learn about what this knee can and can't do so that I am better equipped to accept it.

It is also important to have realistic goals. I don't aspire to be back to competitive dance or run a 5k, but I so badly want to be pain free. I want to be able to do more exercise. I know that I have to surrender to God's will, but it is so tough. How can you or I help or inspire anyone going through a trial, though, if we haven't first gone through it ourselves. My current quick prayer from St. Faustina is "Jesus I trust in You." Jesus knows what I am going through, and He is going to use different people and different experiences to help us and to heal us.

The last couple of months I've also really struggled with how to operate in different ordinary situations. For example, my mom and I went for a short walk around the neighborhood, and a neighbor stopped us to talk. We stood in the same spot to chat for about 15 minutes, and my knee was burning really badly. I couldn't tolerate standing still in one spot for that long. I didn't want to be rude and not talk, so I just endured it, but it was so uncomfortable. I couldn't figure out why I have been able to stand around the house to dry dishes or straighten my closet but not tolerate the standing on a walk. I finally realized that I have to take steps every couple of minutes to prevent the pain from getting bad. When I am doing activities around the house, I take constant small steps, so I have to do that when I am outside standing and chatting with people. It was frustrating because I never had to think about it before, but now I do.

I am learning how to make adaptations in various situations such as taking small frequent steps or having to sit and rest more often. They are small and to most people probably won't even be noticeable. I also might not always have to make them, but I do for now. It is hard having patience with it, but I have to remind myself that I have only been walking for two and a half months and that in another year's time I will be so much stronger. I have to be humble and focus on the positive, but rest assured some days are certainly easier than others.

Some things, though, feel just like normal. Being

out on my driveway with my dog and family felt so incredible. Why? Because it was normal and ordinary. Many of my family members commented on how good it was to see me standing and walking around. How normal it was and how happy they were for me. The day was for my brother, but I got so much joy out of it as well.

At this point in my recovery, I thought I wouldn't need to rely on Jesus so much. Which is probably an odd statement for you to read. I thought that at the year point I would be well on my way. In one sense, I am; I am walking. However, in another sense I am just halfway really. I still have struggles, and I still have burning knee pain. My family and I have made countless prayers asking God to take away my knee pain, and it hasn't happened yet. I saw a TV commercial on EWTN where a viewer wrote in saying throughout his 20s and 30s he was in and out of the hospital. He became very discouraged until he watched EWTN where he learned that in Heaven he will get to meet all the souls he saved because of his suffering. Watching this gave me strength. It was a reminder that there is purpose in my knee pain. I certainly don't get it right now, but I need to continue to place my trust in God.

I also want to remind you to look for the good.

Even the greatest evil points back to truth and to God. The Eucharist and the Blessed Virgin Mary are attacked constantly by satanic practices, but that just makes them even more valid. If the devil is attacking something, it points to its truth, it points to its goodness, and it points to the power of God.

If you are working or striving to do something good, the devil is going to throw obstacles in your way to attack it. Why? Because you are following God's will, and you are living light of God's goodness. And he hates that. At times in our human weakness, we can look around and feel that we are alone in our efforts to serve Christ or that He isn't hearing our prayers. The evil voices can sometimes seem much louder. But don't fall for that.

One day I was particularly discouraged from my trauma that I wasn't improving fast enough, and I started giving into discouragement. It was overwhelming, and I felt really helpless and hopeless. So, immediately my mom grabbed her rosary and started to pray it. It took everything I had in me to try to pray it with her. However, during the rosary I had the most beautiful conversation with God, thoughts not audible or visible yet very much divine. I prayed, "Lord I have suffered so much physically, haven't I suffered enough?"

He answered me, "Yes, you have endured the physical part of my passion. I am inviting you to be with me during my mental aspect of the passion. I too was alone. I was rejected; crowds jeered at Me saying many things that were not true. Be with Me. I am with you, right with you. Trust in Me. The Resurrection is coming."

I replied, "But I'm so scared. I don't want this."

He said, "Please, I am right with you. Mary and John were with me at my cross. They are with you, and John and (Christine) Mary are physically with you at your cross. You are not alone."

Jesus through Mary was comforting me during my distress and gave my soul such comfort and hope. He was with me. The saints were with me. My parents, John and Christine Mary, were with me. So, this is a reminder for you, too. He is with you. The saints are with you. And if you look closely enough, I am sure he has sent you at least one person to truly be with you through it all.

It is amazing to look back and think about how I didn't want to pray the rosary that day. I had said it numerous times before and didn't notice any consolation. Sometimes when you pray, you don't notice anything, but even if you don't notice something, that doesn't mean that nothing is happening. I also want to stress again to pray even when you don't feel like it. I didn't feel like it that day, and God blessed me with abundant graces and spiritual truth and comfort. He wants to give it to you, too. You just have to persevere and turn to Him always.

Part 7

Anniversary of the Accident

So whoever is in Christ is a new creation: the old
things have passed away; behold, new things have
come.

~2 Corinthians 5: 17

Today is the day, the anniversary of my accident. I woke up this morning, and I am not sure how to feel exactly. I want acknowledgment, but then every time somebody does acknowledge it, I feel uncomfortable. How do you respond to a loved one when they say they are grateful that you are still alive? It is a strange sensation.

On one hand, yes, I, too, am the most grateful for more time, a second chance, but on the other hand, what I am supposed to be doing with this gift? Is God happy with how I am spending this time? I don't think He is mad, but could I be doing better? Is He disappointed? I find it difficult to balance two truths, God loves us as we are; we don't have to do anything other than just be. Yet at the same time, we are also called to act, to move, and to take action. This whole year my focus has been on recovering, and I still am recovering. I still have knee pain, quad and hip weakness, and fear of driving again; I also can't wait to graduate, to date again, to be more social with friends (once quarantine lifts, of course). This whole year, I have focused on recovering and praying through this recovery. Thanking God every single morning for the gift of another day, offering up my sufferings for special intentions, seeking Him in the simple and in the suffering. Yet, now I feel a shift in my heart.

I still need to work on recovery for another year. I still have some doctor appointments to get through, yet I have the newfound freedom to return to some aspects of my old life. But how? What is my guiding light? Obviously, not turning to sin or vice as I was already not partaking in the culture's idea of being young and single before my accident. I was given a gift. First, I was given an intensified knowledge that I have great purpose and a job still to do. Even more than that, I have a brand-new vision; it was as if I was given a new lens to see even more brightly, to see beneath the surface, to understand the ordinary significance. How do I take this second chance, this new vision and understanding, and how do I apply it for good? What does God want me to do? He has transformed me, and I would like to share that transformation with others.

My accident occurred on May 22, the feast day of St. Rita. She is the patron of impossible cases and of suffering. It is very fitting. One of my family members brought a blessed St. Rita medal to me when I was in the hospital, and I now wear it often. This is another accomplishment, wearing a necklace, because for months I wouldn't wear one due to fear. The closeness around my neck reminded me of the tightening of my seat belt, difficulty breathing, and neck brace from the scene of the accident. Then one day I decided I was tired of not wearing jewelry, so I put it on and was fine. Again, this isn't that big of a deal, but to me it was just another aspect of my life that could return to normal.

If I had to sum up my first year of recovery in one word, I would say "pain." I have a very strong feeling that my second year of recovery in one word will be "frustration." My knee still hurts; I still have muscle weakness; my gait is still off; I can't reach certain things; I get bored of the same exercises and try to do a new exercise and can't. Frustration. Basically, I am free to live my normal life again, but it is difficult as I don't really know what normal is. The last year of my life was kind of on hold plus it was extra strange with coronavirus.

Yet even amidst my running thoughts, I am incredibly grateful. I am grateful for the gift of life, my life. I am grateful for my health. I am grateful that I am spending today with family—that it can be a quiet and simple day compared to the agony I suffered on this day one year ago. I am extremely grateful that I can walk compared to my lying helpless last year.

The biggest blessing of today, my one-year anniversary, is that this is the first day that St. Jude Church started having outdoor adoration, and my mom was able to drive me there. Amidst all my uncertainties, being with Jesus always gives me such great peace. I was able to thank Him for all that He has done for me this year. I wanted to thank Jesus for walking with me during my suffering and giving me a miracle.

Even now, my parents still have different people come up to them and tell them that they are praying for me. A year later. I am honestly shocked every time they tell me, and it happens pretty often. Without giving too many specifics, my mom was at an event, and a lady we haven't seen in years said that she has been keeping me in her prayers this whole time. This woman is not really the cloistered, devout prayer-person type, if you know what I mean. She is a good woman but has more of a tough exterior. When my mom told me that, I was shocked and very deeply moved. I am always so appreciative of prayers because I certainly need them, especially on some longer, tougher days, but it really meant a lot to me that this woman in particular was praying for me even though I haven't seen her in quite a long time. So, you never know who is praying for you or who is rooting for you from afar. They may never tell you, or you might find out by happenstance, but it really highlights the fact that you aren't alone, and some people really do care.

I'm still amazed as I write this that it is actually my story. Sometimes, it seems so close by; other times, it seems long ago. I wish I could go back and tell myself in the depths of fear and pain that God is going to bless me with healing and strength, and that it is coming soon. So, I want to give you encouragement that Jesus is there with you no matter what you are suffering, and goodness is coming.

Part 8

Stepping Forward

Trust in the Lord with all your heart, on your own intelligence do not rely; In all your ways be mindful of Him, and He will make straight your paths.

~Proverbs 3:5-6

The second year of recovering from a traumatic accident brings a new set of challenges. It changes from pain and fear to frustration and insecurity. It is much better than the first year, don't get me wrong, yet pretty much everything feels different, unfamiliar, and unknown. Everyone has long moved on from your accident; many have even forgotten about it. But you haven't. How do you resume normal life? After your world has turned upside down, what is normal? How do you create your life again?

The last year of my life was basically put on hold. I didn't date; I lost touch with some friends; I wasn't able to do much in terms of advancing my career; I forgot what my routine is; I forgot what an ordinary day is; I about forgot where I used to spend my time.

When you don't have a smorgasbord of appointments and unceasing pain, what do you do with your time?

It's not like you can just brush off your shoulders and resume ordinary living. What if people don't understand? How will people treat me? What if I can't keep up, need to sit down, or need to move? What will people think of me not driving yet? What if I'm with people I don't know very well and need to ask for help? What if I stand out as different or weak? What if people are rude? Or what if people are nice but I get frustrated because I can't do something how I like and get upset? Then, I can look just plain crazy. What if you have certain people who keep pushing and nagging at you to get going and start living when you are doing your best to try.

There is no blueprint. I can't find a book called, "How to Restart Your Life After Nearly Dying and Going Through a Year of Rehabilitation Hell." I can't tell you exactly what to do, but I hope to give you encouragement. I want to share some of my joys and frustrations with you because if you are walking a similar road of being healed from a medical diagnosis or if you have a loved one going through this, it can help give you a taste of what is going on in their mind.

Just because I am walking again, or you are now cancer-free, or the worst is behind you, or a lot of time has gone by, does not equate with being able to forget about it, being done, and moving on. We are still healing and trying to heal. It is not old news. It just has a new headline.

I also want to acknowledge here the loss of what used to be. I even feel guilty typing this sentence. How dare I allow myself to miss my old life when I was given a miracle? I can walk. How can I complain? And I'm not trying to complain. But I have such an ache. I wish so badly that I could do one more intense workout. I wish I could jump and leap once more. Dripping sweat. Adrenaline running high. I miss dance; I miss my workout classes. I miss that feeling, that experience. It is not likely I will have it again. I also miss being carefree. Of not having to think about flooring, or accommodations, or how my knee will hold up at events. So, if you're experiencing this ache, too, I am with you. Jesus is with you too.

I also want you to know that people are supporting you, even people that you don't know or don't realize. You are not alone in your struggle. It sounds cheesy, but it is important to let that sink into your soul. Many people have gone through suffering, and sadly many people after you will go through suffering. I know that isn't exactly comforting because it seems so abstract and not your reality. Even though I know two people, my Aunt Kate and Jamie, who have gone through traumatic accidents and made it out to the other side, I didn't know them while they were going through it. But I can bet you a billion dollars that at point one or another they, too, felt frustrated or discouraged. When months went by and I wasn't back to my old self, I had the tendency to think that nobody else was struggling at the same time.

God knew that I needed a physical reminder of this in the beginning. At my second follow-up doctor's appointment (I was still in my wheelchair), I saw a young guy around my age who was also in a wheelchair. I wondered what had happened to him. He noticed me and said, "I feel your pain." We shared a meaningful look of sorrow but also in comfort knowing how the other felt. I was needed to check in, and he got loaded into his car. I never saw him again. I wish I could have; it would have been nice to talk more. I often wonder how he is doing now. I probably wouldn't recognize him now, and I don't think that was the point of that encounter. God was telling me that another young person, around my community, had also been in an accident of some sort and was also dealing with the struggles of being in a wheelchair. If my parents would have left our house five minutes later, I would have missed him. So, you never know who is close by that is also in a similar boat as you are.

A year later, God also knew I needed another reminder. One day in early June, I went for a walk around my neighborhood by myself when these same racing questions plagued my mind. Will I stand out? Will I be able to keep up with other people my age?

Then all of a sudden a sweet, young voice exclaimed, "Hi!"

I turned and saw a cute little girl with a blonde ponytail. She was probably around five years old. I've never talked to her before; I'm not even sure what her name is.

So, I smiled back, waved, and responded, "Hi!"

Then with such sweetness and exuberance she said, "I like you!"

I didn't know how to respond; I was not expecting that.

I recovered quickly, smiled even bigger, and exclaimed, "Thank you!"

She went back to her bicycle, and I kept going on my walk. I thought in my head, "Thank you, Jesus. I needed that."

I think Jesus used that sweet girl to remind me that young children don't care about a bad knee; they love people just as they are. More importantly, He loves me just as I am. I don't need to do anything; I just need to remember how much He loves me and let His light shine forth for others to know and see as well.

Part 9

This Too Shall Pass

And it shall be that everyone shall be saved who calls on the name of the Lord.

~Acts 2:21

Now, I know what you're thinking. Yeah, right. Easy for me to say. If you would have asked me at any point during this year, I would have told you that it was the slowest moving year of my life. When I was non-weight bearing, those days were agony. Each one drug on and on. Watching movies can only be so fun for so long. When I was weight-bearing, it felt like I would never get to walking hands free again. In middle school I thought about being a physical therapist for a career. How ironic. I am SO glad that I didn't do that. Also, I am sure there are fabulous PTs out there, but if you read my experiences (and I didn't include all of them) you can understand my sentiments.

So, what I am saying is that out of all people, I get it. Rough patches seem like they will never end. I kept checking off each month as each one went by desperately hoping that the next one would go faster. And eventually they did. Remember when I saw Jamie in the hospital? And I thought that I would never be like her again, and now I am. So, even if it seems impossible at the time, cling to God for nothing is impossible with Him.

Now, I actually enjoy going to and celebrating events again, and I never thought that would happen either. Last year, my nana turned 80 years old in June, and she postponed her big party until September so that I could go. My Aunt Teresa hosted it, and even though she has a new ranch home, I could barely navigate it. My dad had to lift me up her porch, and I had to sit in her recliner with my leg elevated while the party enfolded around me. All the guests wanted a group photo, and I felt again in slow motion trying to get up from the chair into the dining room. It wasn't a far distance at all, but to me it was. I felt like I was holding it up, but I simply couldn't go any faster. I also got extreme fatigue talking to people at all holidays and events the entire year—so much so that I would have to leave early at times to come back to my quiet room to decompress. I have never experienced it before, but it was like my brain couldn't take all the stimulation of the back and forth conversations.

This is such a contrast to Nana's birthday this year. My mom and I were able to join Nana and a few of her old friends out to lunch at Weaver Ridge, a really nice restaurant on the golf course. I was able to walk in by myself with ease, and I didn't even think about the flooring. I was very steady, and for the first time in a long time I felt extremely confident.

One of my nana's friends asked, "Didn't you have a cousin around your age in a bad accident?"

I answered with a half-smile, "No, that was me."

I was actually really happy that she said that because it meant that I appeared strong and just plain normal. Now granted, it wasn't the same thing as another young person saying it, but I was really grateful for it, nonetheless.

Finally, more places started to open up after all the coronavirus craziness, and I was also able to meet different friends for coffee and lunch. Again, it was just so freeing, and I just enjoyed it so much more than I ever have before. I remember when I met my friend Gabbi for lunch back around Thanksgiving time. We have been friends since kindergarten, and our tradition is to always eat at Panera and go to Jimmy's Bar for drinks. We got attached to Panera in high school because we would meet up there to study or work on projects, and we always saw people from grade school or high school at Jimmy's, which made it fun. I obviously didn't have the physical ability for Jimmy's, so that time around it was just Panera. I was still on my two crutches with the brace, and it was still so difficult to move. My mom had to help me get inside, and while we were about to go inside, another young guy grabbed the door for me and said, "I've been on crutches before. Those aren't easy, hang in there." That, too, was comforting in the midst of discouragement and frustration. I think about my lunch with Gabbi often. How difficult it was. And how different it is now. I can walk in by myself; I can order food by myself; I can carry my tray by myself. I can be ordinary, and ordinary is very exciting.

I hope this gives you a bit of encouragement in whatever you are going through. On some days, even some months, it seems impossible. That whatever it is will never improve, but I am here to tell you that it will. It may last a while, but it will not last forever. Things will improve. And don't believe it because I am saying it. Believe it because God says so.

Part 10

Back Behind the Wheel

They that hope in the Lord will renew their strength,
they will soar on eagles' wings; They will run and not
grow weary, walk and not grow faint.

~Isaiah 40:31

I used to love driving and being on the road. Even as a baby when my parents couldn't get me to go to sleep, they would take me for a drive, and I would fall asleep immediately. The motion of the car was soothing and relaxing to me. Fast forward to learning how to drive at age 15 with my permit… I loved it. I even got my license on St. Patrick's Day, which I thought was super cool at the time. I have always been a good driver, and I still am. I didn't cause the accident. I was going the speed limit; I was driving on the roadway correctly. But because of somebody else's bad decision, it made me lose my confidence. The same motion that relaxed me as a baby now gave me great fear.

Driving again took a lot of courage—courage I didn't possess on my own and had to pray for and continue to pray for each day. I also leaned on other great people in my life to give me the encouragement and support that I needed. I had to rebuild my confidence, which takes time and quite frankly is darn tough.

For several months I had zero desire to drive again. Zero. I felt that I never wanted to do it again. What if I get in another accident? What if I freak out and overreact while driving? What if I get hurt again? The list of racing questions went on. I'm trying to pinpoint when the desire to drive again came back; it was in March around the time I started to walk again. I think because I was healing physically, I was also healing emotionally. So, the desire to drive again came then, but I still didn't want to attempt it for a while. I was fine with the fact that I would try again in the coming months, but it didn't need to be now.

My eventual first step was to start riding in the passenger seat with one of my parents. I started doing this toward the end of May. Prior to this, I would only ever ride in the backseat because I felt safest there. I then started sitting in the driver's seat with the car turned off in the garage. Through doing this repetitively for weeks, I was finally ready to practice driving in a parking lot. On June 5th, I woke up and felt a deep sense of peace. I told my parents I think I want to drive today. They were shocked because prior to this day, I had told them that I didn't want to try until the fall. My dad drove me to a parking lot near our house. I got into the driver's seat, and I drove for the first time. I thought I would be nervous, but I mainly felt excited and carefree. I just drove around in circles and did some different parking, backing up, etc. The peace that I had felt in the car prior to the accident came back. I felt safe and secure.

Two days later, I went back to that same lot, and I felt very at ease with driving slow in circles and parking. I thought I was ready to try accelerating. This was difficult for me. My old vehicle was very old and because of that I had to press down on the accelerator with a decent amount of force to get it moving, but now practicing on my dad's new car, it accelerates fast with little pressure. This was an adjustment because I got a sinking feeling in the pit of my stomach every time I accelerated. It was the same sensation of being on a roller coaster. So, I practiced accelerating again and again. I only got up to about 25 miles an hour because the parking lot is only so big. I went back to this parking lot a few times, and then I felt ready to drive by myself from my house to St. Jude, which is about a five-minute drive.

That first drive to St. Jude was amazing. Was I

nervous? Yes, absolutely. But I also felt so excited at the same time. It has been my home parish since 6th grade, and I feel so bonded to it. St. Jude is where I learned how to ride a bike (way before 6th grade, FYI!). I completed CCD there and was confirmed through St. Jude's CCD program. I was also the confirmation sponsor for my two sweet cousins, Megan and Molly, through St. Jude's CCD program. It's where I've made countless adoration visits. It's where my parents got married and maybe one day I will as well. It was the perfect place for my first solo drive. Adoration unfortunately wasn't happening that day, so instead I made a stop by the Marian grotto.

I continued to increase my driving distance each day. It was difficult, especially accelerating. Going 45 miles an hour made me super queasy. I was definitely nervous and felt wiped out each time I came home from driving somewhere. But the point here is to persevere. It isn't a race to get back to normal. One day I am confident that I won't be nervous or tired out anymore. That day isn't today, but I am working toward it.

I want to highlight the importance of breaking down fear and not letting it stop you from living. Again, easier said than done. If someone would have told me in May to get behind the wheel and drive around town, I wouldn't have been able to do it. No way. This probably depends on the individual's personality and the level of trauma they have experienced, but for me I would have frozen. I needed to gradually work my way back into driving. For those who can jump right into fearful situations, I'm jealous of you; for those who need to take more time to work through it, that is 100% okay. You aren't on a timetable. It is important to push yourself but at the time and pace that you are comfortable with and ready for.

Part 11

A Chapter on Romance

Love is patient, love is kind. It is not jealous, is not pompous, it is not inflated, it is not rude, it does not seek its own interests, it is not quick-tempered, it does not brood over injury, it does not rejoice over wrongdoing but rejoices with the truth. It bears all things, believes all things, hopes all things, endures all things. Love never fails.

~1 Corinthians 13:4-8

Now, before all my guy readers take off and skip this section, you should know that this chapter isn't about a fairytale. I didn't find my Prince Charming, more like a lot of frogs. So, if you'd like to find out about a lot of crazy guys, keep reading.

It starts off with my devastating heartbreak. A month before my accident, I was dumped by my serious boyfriend. Let's call him Richard.* Now Richard and I were in love, so I thought. He gave me his class ring as a promise ring that we were going to get engaged at about four months into our courtship. He asked me to pick out what kind of engagement ring I wanted around month six of dating. For those curious, I want a big, square-shaped diamond. He promised me that he would be proposing during summer 2020. Instead, I got dumped and suffered a car accident. Yay me.

In April of 2019, he dumped me via an insanely long string of text messages. I was extremely crushed to say the least. He contacted me again after my accident happened and asked if he could stop by to see me. I thought maybe after the thought of him almost losing me would change his mind. He brought me a dead daisy that he picked out of someone's yard as my "get well flowers" and wanted advice for his job. He came by a couple of times, and he clearly had no interest in me. A few weeks later, he texted me wanting his class ring back. I guess he felt too awful to ask in person. I told him that I couldn't get it because it was upstairs in my room. I couldn't do stairs at the time. He said he needed it immediately in case he had to move, so my mom had to go upstairs to find it and stick it in our mailbox for him. He tried contacting me a few other times over the course of several months, and I told him that I saw no point in that. He wasn't there at my cross, so he isn't going to be in my life in the future.

So, what is a girl to do when she gets dumped? Get online! I decided to try out CatholicMatch since I had heard positive experiences about it. This was before my accident. I matched with a few great guys, including my ER doctor, ha-ha. After my accident happened, two guys sent me flowers and one sent me a care package. It was very sweet, and I will always be so appreciative of the gestures.

One memorable first Friday visit, Father Henehan came walking into my room holding a bouquet of red roses. I was kind of weirded out thinking what in the world…

He immediately piped up, "These aren't from me!"

"Well, who are they from?" I inquired half laughing, half wondering.

"I have no idea; I found them on your porch," he answered laughing.

"Thanks for bringing them inside, Father," I said laughing back.

I later looked to see who they were from once Father had left (I didn't need to make it more awkward!). It was a guy, Matthew,* from Catholic Match! I am not getting sponsored by them, but I feel like I should be a spokesperson for them. This guy ended up sending me numerous bouquets of flowers—at least six of them—mainly roses which are my favorite. One was numerous red roses with white baby's breath in a huge vase from a local florist, and it cost over $100. While I loved the flowers, this guy was way too pushy and assumed we were an exclusive couple after one date. I even received what I would describe as a love letter from him, which kind of freaked me out.

There was another guy, Philip,* who was messaging me a bit before my accident. When I was in the hospital, I told him about my accident and what had happened, and his reply was, "Sometimes catastrophic shit happens." That certainly is one way to look at it, but when I was in the middle of excruciating pain, I didn't find it funny. Bye bye, Philip.

After a couple months of communicating with these different guys, I knew I couldn't continue. As you read previously, I was in so much pain that I just didn't have anything to give to any of these guys. I was too exhausted, in too much agony, and I didn't trust my ability to make good decisions in this kind of head space. So, I didn't date for close to one year. It's not that I didn't want to date, but I knew I couldn't. I couldn't walk. I had so much pain, fear, and insecurity; it just wasn't feasible.

Once a year had gone by and I finally gained confidence with walking again, I started to contemplate dating again. As I mentioned in previous chapters, I had difficulty trying to figure out how to start "living" again—meaning being more social with new friends (not people I already know super well, obviously) or going on dates. Basically, having fun and experiencing new things seemed foreign now. I was very terrified to be 100% honest. Not because I didn't want to do it, but because I wasn't sure what it would look like now. What if they don't want to pick me up and drive? What if I'm rusty at striking up new conversation? I guess I wasn't sure how to "be myself" when I felt that I was trying to figure out who my new self is.

Before going on my first date post-accident, my mom told me, "Cait, you are not defined by this accident. You are defined by who you always were and still are, Cait Crowley. Yes, a terrible accident happened to you, but you are much more than that. You have a lot to offer, and you are still the same person you always have been, and now you also have another dimension to you."

Are you curious how my first post-accident date went? Well, it was both awful and amazing at the same time! He seemed to have it all on paper: a strong Catholic (at least supposedly), a great job where he will be a good provider someday, good-looking, and living 10 minutes away from me. What could go wrong? Well, I went out with him two days in a row and received multiple negative comments all evening long. Woo-hoo. He said he doesn't date blondes (bro, I have highlights) but said he'd overlook it. I was told I'm too bubbly and a social butterfly but then in the same breath said I'm too serious and not smiling enough at him. He said he liked that I could have deep conversations but put down how I also like to be light-hearted. He also tried to blame me for why we didn't have a table yet at the restaurant (it was packed with a wait list!) and snapped at me when I didn't know exactly where to park. For anonymity purposes, I won't continue on, but these were a few of many "compliments" that I received. And I got sunburnt on the second date, which was just ironic symbolism of the whole thing.

I told him that I didn't want to continue dating, and the crazy part was that he showed up at mass the next weekend! I was with my mom, dad, and nana as I usually am, and I had forgotten that I told him my usual Mass time. I didn't notice him in Mass, but apparently my mom saw him walk past me leaving the church. I got into the car with my family, and I exclaimed, "Omg, that's Paul!*"

He was in the parking lot, and he waved at our car as we drove past. My jaw literally dropped; I was stunned. You can never predict these guys!

I feel like the old me would have been sad, gotten my feelings hurt, and been disappointed on how the dates with Paul turned out. Instead, I actually found it uplifting. As soon as I came home from that second date, I had a surge of confidence. Why? First, because I defended myself. I have been told that I can be spunky, and that sure came in handy on those dates. But more than that, I navigated getting in and out of his car. I navigated parking lots, the restaurant, and coffee shop. I was able to stand for over 30 minutes waiting for our table! And I did all of it without a family member or close friend. I was able to confidently do all this with somebody new and the fact that I could do it gave me such a boost in confidence.

I felt God's grace pouring down on me and that He wanted me to keep on living and to experience such great joy. He doesn't want me to stay in that place of fear, doubt, and second guessing. He wants me to have fun. He wants me to be happy. And He wants that for you. You may not be in this place now. You may still be in the trenches, and that is okay. Come back to this part when you are healed and ready to move on but are scared like how I was. God will equip you to get through anything, and He will also equip you to move forward when you are ready. It might not be dating for you. Maybe it's going to networking events, getting a new job, becoming more active in the community, volunteering, or going to your grandkid's soccer games. Whatever living is for you. I was a nervous wreck before I went on my dates. I did think I liked the guy, but more than that, it was all those fears. So, don't be surprised if before you begin, you may get anxious, think you can't do it, or aren't ready yet until another year goes by, but I encourage you to try. Talk it over with a family member or close friend and have them be there cheering you on until you are ready to fly on your own. You can do it! You just need to have faith in God's providence.

After I resumed socializing, dating, and basically regaining my life back, I was faced with more tough medical news to swallow...

Part 12

Keeping the Faith
Even When You Get Bad News

But we hold this treasure in earthen vessels, that the
surpassing power may be of God and not from us. We
are afflicted in every way, but not constrained;
perplexed, but not driven to despair; persecuted, but
not abandoned; struck down, but not destroyed.
~2 Corinthians 4:7-9

It's July now, 14 months post-accident. The good news is that I am walking so much faster now. Unfortunately, I am still having chronic burning pain. However, I did finally get to meet my primary orthopedic trauma surgeon. He was a super smart, approachable, kind man. He took a very long time with my mom and me to explain everything and answer every question we had. I was hoping for some answers, and boy did I get them.

Again, I am only 14 months out, only 25 years old, and I already have arthritis in my left knee. There isn't much cartilage left on one side of the knee where it took most of the impact, so now I have close to bone on bone. The cartilage functions as "shock absorber" and a cushion between the bones. When the cartilage deteriorates, one is left with bone on bone. This is why it is so painful, and the doctor expects my pain to get worse with time.

The first thing I am going to try is to use a new custom brace that pushes more of my weight to the outside part of my knee that still has really good cartilage. I am hoping that this is a big improvement and buys me more time. The next thing is for the surgeon to remove the hardware in my knee. Some patients find relief with this; however, I will have to be non-weight bearing and back in physical therapy again. That can sometimes take patients another year or so to recover. Ultimately, I will be given a partial knee replacement. Surgery, non-weight bearing, and physical therapy again. Basically, I am looking at a year or two more to totally recover once all this takes place. The other aspect is that partial knee replacements don't last forever. Often, older patients can make the partial last about 20 years before needing another one; however, they aren't as active as a young person, so they have less wear and tear on it. I would probably need one every 10 years.

To be honest, I didn't really know how to feel once I was told about what lies ahead. Part of me was glad to be informed of what I have. I was so tired of the physical therapists saying I didn't push myself and that my pain was in my head. I now have physical proof through my x-rays and through my consultation that I have arthritis. So, in that sense, I felt relief. I have a name of what it is, and I know what my options are. Knowledge is power. On the other hand, it was depressing news to hear. I didn't want to think about a knee replacement until old age or at least not for a long time. I could potentially have a partial knee replacement at 26, 36, 46, 56, 66, 76, and 86. That would be seven years of recovery, plus another year of the removal of the hardware. I could face eight years of pain and recovery. That makes me sick to my stomach.

I plan to tough it out and push it off as long as I can possibly endure. Hopefully with the help of the brace, I will continue without it for several more years. More importantly, I am praying for a miracle. I got more Holy Water from Lourdes, and I am going to pray every single day that the Lord miraculously grows new cartilage in my knee and that my pain totally goes away. I am going to keep fighting through prayer and not give up on my hope to be totally healed with no more surgery. At times, I have to give myself a pep talk because it seems impossible, and I have to accept God's will. However, I am clinging to Jesus. I am asking in Jesus' name to be healed, and as you read this, I would like to ask for your prayers as well.

I also need to remember the bigger picture. I still have knee pain because God is still doing good through it. That answer may sound anticlimactic upon first reading, but if you think about it, my pain still has purpose, and that means that God is still presently acting and using it for good right here and now. The prayers of suffering people are more efficacious. Why? Because Jesus' prayers and His will were most efficacious when He was suffering on the cross.

This means that He is still using my pain for my own interior growth (which has grown exponentially), for the different people I pray for each day (gives the prayers more weight), and for all those around me (through witness and interaction).

It is not that God isn't hearing my prayers for a miracle, and it's not that He won't ever grant it either. It means that I will have it until it no longer does any more good—even if you can't, and I often can't, see the good coming from it. Do not forget for one second that there is great good.

Part 13

Seeking Hope in the Darkness

For I know well the plans I have in mind for you,
plans for your welfare and not for woe, so as to give
you a future of hope.

~Jeremiah 29:11

I remember being upset with God. Why did the pain have to last so long? Why couldn't I have been healed quicker? Why couldn't I have nicer health care workers? Why couldn't this have been easier? I don't think I will fully know the answers to my questions this side of Heaven; however, I think it was to open my eyes.

The unknown is tough. We don't like it. Or at least a lot of us don't. How are we supposed to deal with the uncertainty? Well, just know that you are in good company. Think of Our Lady. She was given a pretty monumental job, becoming the Mother of God, and after the angel told her, he departed from her. Wait a second, can't she ask some more follow-up questions? Or think of the 12 apostles. They in a sense were like entrepreneurs in a start-up. They didn't have a clearly defined job description when they first started to walk with Christ. They were given an "innovative idea," or rather a person, Jesus and His Church—a radically different way and purpose of life—and they had to go get others to join them. They didn't know what was ahead.

And neither do we. God asks us to follow Him and asks us to trust Him as He leads us where He wants us to go.

There is the old joke that you shouldn't pray for patience because God will send you many opportunities to practice it. Well, I didn't pray for patience, but that was a fruit of the Spirit that I had to learn during this time. I wanted to walk so badly. I wanted to be healed so badly. Yet, the Lord was asking me to sacrifice. Not as a punishment, but for spiritual growth. It reminds me of John 9, 1:3. "As he passed by he saw a man blind from birth. His disciples asked him, 'Rabbi, who sinned, this man or his parents, that he was born blind?' Jesus answered, 'Neither he nor his parents sinned; it is so that the works of God might be made visible through him." Perhaps God is permitting your suffering so that His glory can be seen through you.

Upon reflection, my prayer life greatly shifted

during my time of trial in the unknown. I now see that every action that occurs in my day is an encounter with God. I know that before this accident I had faith. I know that I knew that God was real, that Jesus established His Catholic Church. I know I knew that it was good to pray, go to adoration, say the rosary, and thank God when good things happened to me or to help me do well. I also know that God did not cause my car accident. He didn't wake up and say, "Caitie, better enjoy your day today cause the next several months are going to suck." No. He may have permitted it so I could grow in hope. Also, one can never have the attitude of 'okay I got faith, check. Now, I have hope, check.' It is a continuous process of improvement on increasing faith, hope, and love over a lifetime.

Now that I'm several months out from the accident, I think I needed an increase in hope. I knew God was all powerful, and He could do whatever He wanted to but not necessarily that He would for me. I needed to push myself and work to get what I wanted, which isn't bad necessarily, but I think I tried to fit God into what I was wanting. My old wants are laughable—jobs, school, dating, etc. I wasn't truly focusing on the true meaning of life. But, I now need to see God in every moment of every day. I need to wake up every day and say how is my soul? How is my relationship with God? The tasks we do each day don't matter in and of themselves but rather their deeper meaning does. Even mundane tasks can become a powerful prayer if offered to God. Getting back to faith, hope, and love are important. I think God wanted to use this accident to purify me and refine my faith. It was a reset like, 'Hey!!! Trust in the Lord. If He can spare your life and make your body new as if nothing happened, He can bring you through the darkness.' Hope can grow within me, which then allows the Holy Spirit to work more through me because I can more freely cooperate with His will.

I also want to remind you that God does not cause evil or wish evil things to happen to us; however, they occur because of our fallen nature and free will. So, He uses it to bring good. Can He stop things from happening? Yes, of course, but He sometimes permits it for our own good, for our salvation. Again, He doesn't cause any of it. That being said, it can be used as a means of purification so that we realize everything that happens in our lives minute to minute is a gift from God. His will is unfolding amid boring mundaneness as much as thrilling excitement. Trials teach us that we don't earn God's love by doing good things, although we should still do good things, but that His love is given to us freely. So, we need to realize that our faith doesn't rely on what we do like going to mass, check, prayed, check, but on Him alone. When we cannot rely upon ourselves to fix something, we realize that we must rely solely upon Him. It is easy to fall into the trap of relying upon ourselves and squeezing God to fit within the container we create for Him. Everything is a gift from God. If you learn that and put your sole dependence on Him, you won't be disappointed.

Remember when things are going your way that it is the Lord who is blessing you; when things are not going your way, it is the Lord inviting you to trust Him. It's like a parent teaching a toddler to walk. If the parent never takes a step back from the child, the child cannot take a step forward. But just like an attentive parent, His arms are always there to catch you.

Part 14

Hanging On and Letting Go

*There is an appointed time for everything, and a time
for every affair under the heavens...A time to seek,
and a time to lose; a time to keep, and a time to cast
away.*

~Ecclesiastes 3:1,6

Each day the clock keeps ticking, and each day we
have the chance to grow. I am now many months
post-accident, and I am continuing to work on healing and strengthening myself, physically, mentally,
emotionally, and spiritually. While I am not "done," I
am so proud of where I am overall.

I am so grateful to have my life back, and I am also
so grateful for the summer I have had, in particular
the Fourth of July. This year on the 4th, I reflected on
how my life looked this time last year. My dad had
cooked our food, and we had my nana over for dinner.
I wore a cute red, white and blue top to try to get in
the spirit, but my pain was so bad, it didn't really
matter. My mom wheeled me into the kitchen. I nor-

mally talk to my nana for hours, but the pain engulfed me. I physically felt so weighed down. I couldn't tolerate sitting upright to eat. I tried to push through the pain to try to talk, but I simply could not. I cried, apologized, and said I have to lay down, the pain was burning. My nana understood and left. Happy Independence Day, where I felt anything but independent.

This is in total contrast to July 4, 2020. I could walk, I could drive, I could celebrate, I could laugh. This year I had such a deep peace, and I didn't even do anything particularly exciting. This year, I am independent again, thanks to the healing power of God. The day of the accident could have been the total end for me, but it wasn't. The day of the accident could have been a permanent, life-long battle of deep suffering, but it wasn't. The day of the accident was the day God saved me, tangibly showed me His love, and walked with me through the deepest darkness I've ever experienced. It was a pivotal moment in my life.

After all this spiritual, mental, emotional, and physical growth, though, a fear of mine is forgetting. I remember Father Henehan explaining during one of our talks that when I am 40 years old, a lot of this experience will fade. He said I will obviously remember that I was in a bad accident and couldn't walk, but a lot of the specifics will become fuzzy. At the time he said this, I thought that seemed crazy! I was confident that I would always remember everything because it was so awful. Now that some time has passed, however (don't worry I'm still only 25 years old, not 40), I can already start to see that becoming true. Some moments I don't think about much anymore, but on occasion something triggers my memory. On one hand, I want some of these memories to fade. I don't think it's healthy to dwell on negative past events; on the other hand, I don't want all the goodness and growth to be forgotten.

So, how do you keep perspective? How do you not dwell on the past and get out of the patient viewpoint? Yet at the same time, how do you remember what is important? How do you remind yourself that whatever is annoying you now isn't that big of a problem?

One suggestion is to have a physical, tangible reminder that is associated with the past but has a positive emotion attached to it. For example, I had my mom video record my walking every two months. This helped me to see my progress, and it was really cool to run all the videos together to see how strong I was becoming. While it is sad to think how I was in the first video, it is empowering to see where I am in the last video. Whenever I start fretting about some-

thing unimportant like I was late to work or the grocery store was out of my favorite food or whatever, I
am going to watch my videos to remind myself this
stuff isn't important. I have my faith and my health
and will keep perspective.

I also recommend having a "holy reminder" as
Mother Angelica called them. This is a religious item
of some sort. I like to wear a cross, blessed miraculous
medal, or blessed saint medal (shout out to St. Rita)
on a necklace. It could be a small picture or image of
Jesus put in your car or office. It could be carrying a
rosary in your pocket. Whatever you like that reminds
you of God. Everyone needs to be reminded of God
whether they go through a trauma or not. It is
important to have a holy reminder nearby even if you
don't wear it all the time because then you visibly see
it, and it can remind you to look up.

I also believe in letting go as well. God lives in the
present moment. He was there in our past and will be
there in our future, but to Him it is ever present. And
that is where He asks us to live, in the present. I once
had a whole basket full of cards that people had sent
me over the course of my recovery. On tough days, I
would read them to remind myself that people cared
and were praying for me. However, once a year
passed, I was ready to let go of them. They had pro-

vided comfort when I needed them, but I was ready to move on. I was ready for birthday cards and new text messages; I no longer wanted to read about the accident. I believe this is healthy and showed that I had healed. I still truly appreciate every single card I ever received. I still know who those people are and hold them close in my heart, but I don't need to keep the cards in order to keep the good deeds. God wants us to be alive now, and it is important to strike a balance between remembering the good and letting go at the same time.

Part 15

Unexpected Blessings

I am the vine; you are the branches. Whoever remains in me and I in him will bear much fruit, because without me you can do nothing.

~John 15: 5

I want to take a moment to let you know why I decided to write this book and share my thoughts because originally I didn't want to. My nana had been telling me for weeks how she thought I should write a book, and, to be honest, I thought it sounded crazy. A whole book? Where would I begin? It sounded kind of daunting, and I wasn't sure that I wanted to be vulnerable. Nobody wants to read a book about someone who doesn't open up, and it's tough to open up. There were moments that I didn't really ever want to have to think about again.

I mentioned earlier that I have a close relationship with Deacon Roger and his wife because they were my 8th grade CCD teachers and brought me Communion every Sunday while I was homebound. Well, one night, Deacon Roger messaged me on Facebook's Instant Messenger asking how I was doing, and I was super exhausted, so I decided to respond in the morning (sorry if you end up reading this!). I messaged him an update on my health, and then turned off my phone because I had to jump on a video call with my marketing agency. This was the day that I found out my contract was not going to be renewed because of coronavirus. I expected it but still was a little bummed out.

I went back to look at my phone and saw this message from Deacon: "Are you working on your book? You have a very inspiring story to tell. Not just what happened but about faith and trust in God. A lot of people need and would like to read such stories. That's the one regret I have so now it is a lot more work plus my memory is going. Do it!"

I again was hesitant and gave a non-committal response. He replied, "I encourage you to proceed! You have quite a story, and it can help many! It's like the Good News, you cannot keep it hidden!"

After receiving that message, I felt urged by the Holy Spirit to write. And so I did. I wrote for three and a half days straight and completed the core of my book. Since then, I have added more content. I really felt God was working through Deacon to nudge me to do this. I am imperfect; my book is imperfect, but I hope that it can help people during challenging times and can lead people closer to Christ.

What is somewhat ironic about this whole experience is that I have always struggled with putting my total trust in God. It's like tearing off flower petals and saying, "I trust You, I trust You not" instead of saying, "I love you…I trust You." I wanted to trust Him, but I let that doubt creep in because of past negative experiences. In a lot of ways, I don't really feel equipped to be writing about trust in God because I've struggled so much with it. God has given me such support and encouragement, yet I still panic.

I have often identified with the passage regarding the disciplines on the boat when Jesus is asleep. It's like "Wake up, Jesus!!! Everything is falling apart!!! Might be a good time to step in here!!!" However, in hindsight, learning to have total trust in God has really been at the core of this journey. When terrible things are happening to me, I have to trust that God is with me, that He will bring me something 10x better in the future, and, in the meantime, He will be walking with me through the storm. I encourage you to say this throughout every day when doubt or worry starts to creep in, "Jesus, I trust in You."

Think of when a landscape architect is creating a new backyard for someone. Perhaps he or she plants a new tree; it is small and doesn't appear to provide any value. You have to nurture it and give it time to take root and grow. Eventually, it will turn into something beautiful. It will provide shade, color, vibrancy. And you can't forget that the tree is a part of a bigger picture, the entire backyard beauty. It is in the small that we, too, can become beautiful. We can add beauty to a bigger picture.

Part 16

Share Your Story

Always be ready to give an explanation to anyone
who asks you for a reason for your hope.

~1 Peter 3:15

Hope. There is such a lack of it in today's world. It seems like some people have it made and everything goes their way while others can't catch a break and suffer greatly. At times, it is honestly easier to give in to discouragement than to hope because you can't see how it is fair or how you will get through this. This is why sharing your testimony is so important. Our Lord is calling you and me to do this; however, it will look different for each individual and each situation.

Since my accident, I have heard about two women who are close to my age, who live in my community, and who have been in horrific car accidents. I'm single, one is a single mother, and one is married. While we all live in the same community, the odds are that I wouldn't have ever connected with them except through our shared trauma. I reached out to both of them to give hope after hearing about their accidents. I shared with them that I went through the same pain and anguish but that I made it and they will make it, too. I believe it brought them both consolation. I want to be like Jamie to others that I encounter in the future as well.

During my journey, I have also stayed close with Jamie as I have mentioned before. When hospital restrictions let up from coronavirus, we plan to visit trauma patients together in the hospital. We want to help pay it forward and share our stories to help bring encouragement. We hope that our suffering can bear fruit by bringing comfort and hope to others. #TeamTraumaSurvivors. I again want to encourage you if you have gone through suffering to reach out to somebody around you who is now going through the same thing. It can bring so much hope and strength to those who desperately need it, and it will mean so much more coming from you because you have been in their shoes.

It is also important to share your story with others who haven't been through this experience as well. They can learn from you. Maybe everything is going their way now, but they or someone they know may go through suffering in the future, and they can reflect back on your conversation. You can also be a reminder to them to be grateful for the life that they have now. I have found that this is much tougher for me because some people won't seem to care too much or will brush over it. And if they do, then just accept it. I am not saying to share your entire life story with everyone you interact with, but at times when it is appropriate, be courageous in sharing a snippet of your story and point back to God. He will provide you with opportunities and give you a nudge when you need to speak. All you have to do is be willing to cooperate with Him.

It is also critical to continue intercessory prayer. I try to continue to pray every day for those who are suffering, and when I know of someone specific, I offer up my lingering knee pain for them. I recently went to get coffee with my sweet cousin, Molly. I was on a high because I was able to drive myself, be independent, and spend time with my cousin. While I was there, I saw a man in a wheelchair drinking coffee alone, and my heart was very saddened for him. I'm sure that he wanted to get out and get a change of scenery, and I'm glad he did. But I was so sad that not only was he in a wheelchair, but he was also alone with no one to chat with. I tried not to stare and tried to smile. I wanted to say something to him, but I didn't know what to say that wouldn't be awkward. Instead, I said a quick prayer for him in that moment, and I offered up my pain of the next day for him. I don't say this to get kudos; I am asking you to do the same.

You may share your testimony, or someone may share it for you. Father Henehan shared with me that one of St. Jude's parishioners was homebound and suffering from a medical condition. Father visited him monthly to bring him First Friday Communion. He shared with this man that he was trying to get nuns for St. Jude to teach at our grade school and be a part of our parish life. Hundreds of parishes around the U.S. were applying to bring them to their parish, so this man said he would offer up his pain and suffering every single day that St. Jude would get them. This went on for months of back and forth until one First Friday. That man told Father, "We got the nuns." Father was surprised and said he was still waiting an answer. Later that day, Father got the call from the order that they were coming to St. Jude. So, that man knew before Father knew! Shortly after finding out about the nuns, that man passed away. What a testimony to the importance of offering up our pain and suffering.

My outlook on life has completely changed and been transformed, and I can't help but think I was spared to help share the Gospel in a different way. I am not a theologian nor am I trying to be. However, my accident is an example of how to live the Gospel in the twists and turns of life, how to cope and navigate the darkness of suffering, and how to count on God to address every single fear, doubt, or question you may have. As I mentioned earlier on, suffering well bears great fruit, and sharing your story is one way to help spread hope to a world that desperately needs it.

Part 17

Call to Action

If you understand this, blessed are you if you do it.
~John 13: 17

If you have been moved by my story, I would like to invite you to take action in very simple, easy ways.

Business owners. Some of you are doing wonderfully. Others of you know that your parking lots are disintegrating and that you have no flat surfaces or entryways, no elevators, no railings, and no process in place for those needing special accommodations. I have encountered all of these issues just within my hometown, and I am very confident that this happens all over the country. Please make improvements.

One business in town is located in an old building with a winding staircase with no elevator. That is a violation and could be grounds for being shut down. Another business in town has physically barricaded their handicap accessible entrance because "too many people were sneaking in that way;" so they make all their customers climb a steep incline to get to the other area of the facility. This incline also has disintegrating concrete. I talked with a manager, and she didn't want to budge at first. My family let them know that legally they have to provide accommodations, or they will be in violation, so they begrudgingly found someone to unlock the front gate. These are just two of several institutions that I've encountered who don't either have or want to have accommodations. It is mostly small- or medium-sized places that think they won't be caught.

I and many others could hire lawyers and sue these places, but that shouldn't be necessary. I'm asking businesses to change for two reasons: One, it's the right thing to do. Two, it will pay off with happier employees and more satisfied customers. People will be more likely to patronize your business, and they will also tell others to patronize your business. This will also benefit the elderly and small children who also can easily trip or fall. There are many great incentives for you, including the fact that it could be a great marketing tool.

There have been tons of marches going around the U.S. right now and for good reason. But I want to point out that it isn't likely that you will see individuals with disabilities marching through the streets.

Why? Because they physically don't have the ability to do that. People who march are individuals who are blessed with a good body and strong stamina. Like I said, my cross was temporary, but God gave me this experience for a reason. I have such an eye-opening, first-hand experience of what it feels like to be discriminated against because I physically can't navigate cheap construction. Every human person has dignity and should be able to go to places in the community just like anyone else. My money is the same as anyone else's money. It is such an injustice.

If you know some people who own a business, ask them and encourage them to improve their property structures and improve their processes. How hard is it to unlock a door you already have? How hard is it to have someone repair old concrete? How hard is it to put in a chair lift or escalator? This is not about highlighting these individuals over someone else; it is about providing everyone equal access to the same experiences.

Individuals can help, too. If you are with someone or even if you just notice someone struggling to get somewhere, offer to help. Maybe it is holding their hand so that they can balance getting up a step. Maybe it is holding the door open so that they can focus on just simply walking. Maybe it's pointing out to a business owner that something is broken or a trip hazard. Be an advocate. This is done not by shouting from the rooftops but simply when the opportunity unfolds in front of you, please respond. God is giving you a chance to show love and compassion to someone, and you are helping to encourage and strengthen the individual. It will probably only take a few seconds and at most a few minutes, so why not? Perhaps if you do so, when the day comes you need help (and that day will come eventually), someone will be inspired to help you.

And for the individual experiencing this first-hand, I understand how tough it is. Not all places are accessible, or they are poorly accessible. I once again want to encourage you to not give up. You deserve to be there just as much as anyone else, if not more. God is close to the broken hearted because He identifies with it so closely. Think about it. How many times a day does God offer His heart and His love, and how many times a day does He get rejected. We get upset because ONE person rejects us or ONE place isn't welcoming. Millions of people completely reject God every single day through simply being indifferent and having a blah attitude of "I'm good and don't need God." Then think about how deeply His heart is wounded by those who put Him down by saying He doesn't exist or by making fun of Him. Then think about us who try to love Him but in our humanity fail Him despite our best and most sincere efforts. God is close to the broken hearted because He knows that pain well and wants to draw you close. Remember that God knows that pain, but He also knows His love for you. All you have to do is choose to receive it.

I never realized any of this and never thought about any of this until my accident. I have always been in great shape and took it for granted. Like I mentioned early on in this, I never thought that I wouldn't have my physical health until old age. Never crossed my mind once. So, I felt compelled to write this chapter—not to shame or slam businesses (I am pro-business; my undergraduate degree is in business!) but for awareness. I think some people get so busy with their lives that they don't stop to think about the bigger picture. So, if one business or one person decides to make improvements so that individuals don't have to be singled out, don't have to call ahead of time or struggle in any additional way, then this has been worth it.

Part 18

What is the Meaning of Suffering?

For this momentary light affliction is producing for us an eternal weight of glory beyond all comparison, as we look not to what is seen but to what is unseen; for what is seen is transitory, but what is unseen is eternal.

~2 Corinthians 4:17-18

Before I even begin to try to give my thoughts to this question, I highly want to encourage everyone to read St. Pope John Paul II's Apostolic Letter on Human Suffering, SALVIFICI DOLORIS. It contains within it much wisdom and gave me great peace. Through my rehabilitation journey, prayer, and St. JP II, I have grown exponentially in understanding why suffering exists and its purpose for us.

I never understood why Jesus had to suffer. Why the passion and crucifixion? How was it fair that Jesus, so gentle, so perfect, so loving, why Him? Why would the Father let Him go through all of that?

Couldn't there be another way?

Through prayer and reading St. JP II's writing, I was given an insight by the Holy Spirit. Because only the Son of God, God himself, could have the ability to defeat evil, He had to come to earth. Sin, death, and suffering are a result and a consequence of evil. Jesus had to strike evil at its core in order to defeat it. And to defeat it, he had to undergo it and sanctify it. It makes logical sense when you look at the depth that is often hard to see. It had to be accomplished the way in which it was, through the crucifixion, because the spiritual dimension realities of sin, death, suffering, and ultimately evil had to be crushed through God's power.

The Father wills it not because He wants to see His son suffer and go through torture and agony, but He permits it for the greater good—the salvation of the world. Jesus accepted it for love of the Father and for love of us. So, if Jesus's suffering was for the salvation of the world, our own sufferings are for our own personal salvation and those around us. God asks us to accept our sufferings for love of Him. Acceptance does not mean wishing for it or liking it but rather a continual turning toward God. Humanity was purified through the sufferings of Jesus, and our own souls can be purified through our own suffering.

I can sometimes find myself being mad at God. Why do I have to have this? Why do I have to go through all this? It can feel like a punishment when in reality it is love. The Father loves us so deeply, more than we can ever probably understand, and because of love, He wants us to be with Him forever, and He knows exactly what needs to happen in our lives in order to get us there.

It is also important to remember that in the beginning, this was never God's plan. Suffering is a result of evil from when Satan turned away from God and got Adam and Eve to do the same. If God removed evil, He would be removing free will and thus the ability to choose whether or not we want to love Him in return. He does not want to take that gift away from us, so instead He sanctifies our suffering and turns evil into great, glorious good. God provides us with the perfect model of how to undergo suffering, Jesus. He is our hope and our strength, and if we press onward, we will rise with Him.

I also never understood how the saints could be joyful in their sufferings. How could years of suffering or facing martyrdom be joyful? Are these people just way more emotionally stronger than I am? Were they just so much holier than I am? I am sure that the saints experienced the same range of human emotions as you and I do. Fear, discouragement, worry, anger, the list could go on. However, instead of focusing on their feelings, they knew deep in their souls that their sufferings were uniting them to Christ. They knew that by partaking in Christ's sufferings, they may also partake in Christ's resurrection.

We also need to remember to ask Mary to pray for us because Jesus shared the most suffering with her. After Jesus, the suffering of her life and in particular the passion, she was able to offer that up, unite it with her son's sufferings as an offering to the Father, for the salvation of the world. Not only is Mary the Mother of God, and not only is she the perfect disciple (I never realized it until now), but she is also a wonderful example of how to suffer well. She united her sufferings to those of Jesus, and she can teach us how to do the same.

I recently realized when we pray the rosary, we are asking Mary to pray for us while the events of Jesus's life are happening. In a mystical way, she can pray for us and unite it to her son during these specific times that hold within them a magnitude of grace. Mary, through the rosary, helps to unite our suffering to her son's suffering. This uniting led Mary to be assumed into Heaven, so we can hope for our personal resurrection one day.

In the Apostolic Letter on Human Suffering, entitled SALVIFICI DOLORIS, St. John Paul II wrote:

In suffering there is concealed a particular *power that draws a person interiorly close to Christ,* a special grace…When this body is gravely ill, totally incapacitated, and the person is almost incapable of living and acting, all the more do interior *maturity and spiritual greatness* become evident, constituting a touching lesson to those who are healthy and normal…Suffering is, in itself, an experience of evil. But Christ has made suffering the firmest basis of the definitive good, namely the good of eternal salvation…

People react to suffering in different ways. But in general, the individual almost always enters suffering with a *typically human protest* and *with the question "why"*. He asks the meaning of his suffering and seeks an answer to this question on the human level…Man hears Christ's saving answer as he himself gradually becomes a sharer in the sufferings of Christ.

Part 19

Ready to Die

For you are dust, and to dust you shall return.
~Genesis 3:19

Going back to what I said in the beginning, nobody really wants to think about life and death. Death is too heavy of a topic. It is much more exciting to hear about exotic travels or the cute new rescue puppy you adopted. While we are meant to enjoy life, we also need to remember that this life is temporary. We are all only here a very limited time, and we have to think of where we want to end up.

In my graduate program, I was enrolled in my final course (minus the capstone project), entitled Persuasion and Strategic Communication. I was really excited about this class because it had a heavy writing focus in it. The first week of class, I got to "meet" my professor on a nearly two hour sync session call where he talked about the class material, expectations, questions, etc. It always took me a couple weeks to get the hang of the rhythm of the class

and what the teacher was looking for. I was just starting to grasp that at the beginning of week two when I
received an email from Northwestern University
informing my classmates and I that my teacher, Mark,
had passed away. My first instinct was shock and then
sadness. I actually was kind of mad at him earlier
because he hadn't answered my email or discussion
board question. Now I know why. I don't know if this
man was Catholic or Christian or anything for that
matter, but I am praying for his soul, nonetheless.

I share my professor's story to remind you that
not everyone makes it to old age and not everyone
gets a forewarning that it's going to happen. There is
a Latin phrase, *memento mori*, which means to
remember your death. Each year on Ash Wednesday
we are told "Remember you are dust and to dust you
shall return." We always need to be ready for eternal
life and live with those phrases in mind. It can be so
easy to get caught up in distractions, goals, or even
suffering that we forget the bigger picture. God wants
us to be with Him in eternal life forever, but it is our
choice whether or not we want to be with Him. He
gave us freewill. He does not force anyone to have a
relationship with Him, but He always wants and
hopes that each of His children comes home to Him.

So, the questions to ask now are: Am I living in

such a way that I would be ready to meet Jesus right now? Am I in a state of grace? Have I frequented the sacraments, especially receiving the Eucharist at Mass and receiving the healing graces of confession? Do I have a daily prayer life?

Am I harboring un-forgiveness in my heart? Have I been showing kindness to my brothers and sisters in Christ? Basically, am I doing everything in my power to choose God and His will on a daily basis?

I have to ask myself these questions every single day. Some days, I can answer with a strong resounding "Yes!" and other days with more of "Uh, I think so." There will be ups and downs in the spiritual life, no doubt, but I believe what God wants to see is an intentional, disciplined effort. Are you showing up even when you don't feel good or when things aren't going your way? Are you staying close to the faith even when it's unpopular? Are you staying close to Jesus even when your path is unclear and you have no idea where He is leading you?

The struggles and pain that God permits us to face are to give us a nudge to return back to Him. Run, don't walk (if you can of course!). The evil one tries to get us to turn away from God in times of trouble. The devil wants us to doubt God's goodness and that he cares and pushes us to discouragement. The devil also tries to get us to turn to vice to make us feel better or to solve our problems. This is a disorientation of a good. We are to turn to God always. In the good and in the bad. He is with us always, and He wants to show us His love. God is the answer to everything.

If you are blessed with the ability to know that you will die in advance, don't see this as God is punishing you or that you have unnecessary suffering. He may be allowing you to suffer here so that you don't have to suffer in purgatory. Also, call a priest as soon as you can to give Last Rites (and hope he does a better job than the hospital priest I had!). I also highly encourage loved ones to pray the Divine Mercy Chaplet for the sick and dying. This prayer takes probably five minutes or less, and I encourage you to read what Jesus revealed to St. Faustina regarding the promises associated with it if someone prays this prayer for the dying.

If you have no warning that you are going to die but you have a few seconds before it happens, similar to what almost happened to me, call upon the name of Jesus and say you are sorry for your sins. If you remember the act of contrition even better, but in a moment of panic, it might leave you. However, even just saying the simple words of "Jesus, I am so sorry for my sins" has so much weight to it. I believe that the Holy Spirit prompted me to say that, and I complied with His will in that moment. It could have very well been the prayer that saved my life, and it could very well be the prayer that saves your soul.

Conclusion

*God not only loves you very much but also has put his
hand on you for something special.*

~Thessalonians 1:4

I hope my story can help you if you ever find
yourself going through a trial, but I really want my
story to inspire you to go deeper into your relationship with God. Have you ever wondered why you are
the way you are?

Every single person reflects an image of Him. God
is scientific. God is mathematical. God is humorous.
God is kind. God is creative. Think of all the good,
positive, joyful attributes—what we call as talents or
characteristics—and know we inherited them from
Our Father.

People say, "Oh, you have your father's eyes" or
"you dance just like your mother." Why, too, then
would we not resemble Our Father who creates our
very essence. Next time someone puts you down,
remember how you reflect a piece of God. Remember
you have value. Your talents, your gifts are a physical

reminder of how you are God's child and made in the image and likeness of Him.

We study in school many wonderful authors throughout all the literature classes, people like Shakespeare, Edgar Allen Poe, F. Scott Fitzgerald, Robert Frost, etc. We are immersed in the story line, characters, syntax, context, symbolism, picking apart of every detail grasping to know more. Why then do we not take the time to read about The Author of Creation, the One who wrote you into existence and the One who helped those writers create the wonderful pieces of work they did. More than read, what if instead you could actually talk to and be in the presence of The Author and form a relationship with Him? Wouldn't you want to do that? We are only on this earth for a short time; we need to make sure that we are ready when God calls us home.

Most importantly, remember that Heaven starts now! Don't live aimlessly for 90 years and then go meet God. Meet Him now, prepare for eternal life now. He is here now! Not somewhere in the distance or up in the clouds. God is everywhere, and He is physically present in tabernacles around the entire world. This should radically change your life. Church isn't an obligation, but a person, Jesus Christ, to love. As I have from the beginning, with the grace of God,

I am taking it one day, one step at a time, and I invite you to do the same.

Bonus Update

It has been two years now since my car accident. Lots of pain, anguish, and tears have turned into radiant joy. I finished my graduate degree with a 4.0 GPA. I received two full-time job offers and accepted an HR communication representative role at a Fortune 100 company, which was the company that I had always wanted. I got my first book published, and I can now go on 40-minute walks. Thank you, Jesus, my life is Yours.

Made in the USA
Monee, IL
15 September 2021

78095674R00089